MW00983812

U.S. History for Beginners

Revised Edition

**Julie Collins with
Richard Bonneville**

Copyright 2023 © by Julie Collins
Copyright 2023 © Cover design by Courtney Steele
Welcome All rights reserved.
ISBN: 9798853172845

AUTHOR DEDICATION

Julie Collins

To Marty Collins for dreaming with me, encouraging me, loving me, and listening to me always. You are my heart and my true love.

To Pete Carroll for believing in me, dreaming with me, and making me the proudest parent on the planet. You are my heart and my driving force.

To Richard Bonneville for countless hours of teaching me History and answering all the questions. Thank you for the laughs, the fun in the classroom, and especially for your friendship. You are a tremendously talented teacher, coach, and a great mentor.

To the many, many ESOL students at May River High School. You inspire me daily and you are the reason I wrote this book. Thanks for the memories. You are my motivation.

Richard Bonneville

To my beloved wife Leah and my cherished family,

I am forever grateful for your unwavering support throughout my journey. In moments when I sought stability, you have been my solid ground, providing strength and encouragement. Your love and understanding have been my guiding light, allowing me to navigate the ups and downs of life.

To Julie Collins,

Thank you for being the catalyst that transformed a mere opportunity into a breathtaking adventure. Together, we have embarked on an extraordinary path, overcoming obstacles with tenacity, and sharing countless unforgettable moments. From the humblest of tasks, like setting mouse traps, to the exhilarating challenges of creating workbooks, projects, and curriculum, you have been a constant source of inspiration and camaraderie.

To the countless ESOL students who have touched my life,

Each and every one of you has left an indelible mark on my heart. Your unwavering passion and burning desire to learn have ignited a fire within me. It is your relentless pursuit of knowledge that fuels my own aspirations to be a better educator and mentor. Your presence has brought me immeasurable joy, and I am eternally grateful.

Background Information:
Learning the Story of The United States of America

In school, I never enjoyed history classes. I always felt so bored with all the never-ending facts and dates that seemed to be a part of this subject. Fast forward many, many years later and I sat in a U.S. History classroom as an adult learner, dreading every minute of what I was about to endure. It was a high school classroom, led by Richard Bonneville, and I only sat there to re-learn history so that I could teach it to my ESOL students. Surprisingly, from the very first day in class I became helplessly engaged in the actual story of America. It was fascinating to me. No teacher had ever been able to get me excited about history before, so I guess you could say he had a special gift of making it interesting. I found myself taking notes, drawing charts upon charts with pictures to teach what I was learning to my students, and even discussing things about what we learned in class at home in the evenings! I was mind-blown with how fascinating our history really was. Now, I'm going to break down what I learned into sections so you can learn it, too.

This book is not meant to go into great detail and depth about American history. You can find that by reading a textbook. This is merely an overview or introduction to the major events in history, things that helped to shape our nation, and give you a general idea of the order in which things occurred. Therefore, this book should pique your interest to dive in deeper to learn more about the subject. Hopefully, you will do that in your U.S. History class and this book will help you to have a general idea of the subject. Important academic vocabulary will be **bold** in the text. There are also questions after each section to answer and possibly some ideas of topics to further explore and research on your own. The way I see it, the more you learn from this book, the better prepared you will be for the actual class when you enroll. The details and depth of U.S. History will come later, so use this as a pre-U.S. History learning guide.

So, where does our story begin? How did we become the United States of America, anyway? Get ready to learn all about the story of how we started with England, how we became independent from them, and how our government was set up. You will learn all about the dreams of the people, the struggles, the hard work, and the ideas of men and women that helped to shape our nation.

There were Presidents and First Ladies, Generals and Judges, and people who came from all over the world who wanted to live here and have a chance at The American Dream. As you work through the sections in this book, you will quickly learn that the people had struggles, hardships, disagreements, extreme wealth, and bitter depression as they fought for what they wanted. Rebellions occurred, agreements were reached, and sometimes the rebellions turned into battles. Sadly, battles developed into wars and many people died, lost their homes, starved, and watched their American Dream fade away as a result.

One thing that is evident in America's history is that the resilience of the people kept the dream of our forefathers alive. Generation after generation of Americans proved that the American Dream was something that many people from all walks of life deeply desired. Many were willing to give up everything to have a chance to achieve the dream. This great nation started from very humble beginnings and progressed through the years to the country we live in today, alive with many different cultures, languages, religions, political beliefs, and a strength that is steadfast and true.

You will learn as you progress through the sections how America has seen many highs and many lows throughout her history. At times you will agree with what occurred, and at other times you will feel outraged at the events that have happened. I would like to thank the only history teacher that was ever able to really teach me this subject, Richard Bonneville. He delivered lessons which resulted in my creating a multitude of charts, lots of disagreements and questions, tons of laughter and fun, and igniting a passion within me for writing this book. He is truly one of the best teachers I've ever worked with, and he deserves recognition for a job well done. So, let's get started, shall we? I'm excited to teach you what I know. Never fear! You will not be bored. With this story, that is impossible.

Happy Learning!

Julie Collins

TABLE OF CONTENTS:

NOTE: These units of study are aligned with the current ***South Carolina State Standards*** for U.S. History.

UNIT 1: FOUNDATIONS OF AMERICAN REPUBLICANISM

Lesson 1.1: The Original Colonies

Figure 1

In the beginning, **England** was in control of America. It was the **17th century**, the 1600's, and England had a lot of money and power. Let's get something straight that can sometimes be confusing. There were already people in America. This land was known as *The New World*. What will be explored in this workbook is how *The New World* became settled into The United States of America. It started with England wanting to make money in *The New World*, so the King wrote orders for important people (called Lords) to go to the land along the East coast to settle and make money there. These orders were called **The Royal Charters.**

You probably already know that America is divided into states. (Georgia, New York, Texas, etc.) Well, back in the 1600's these areas were called **colonies.** There were a total of 13 colonies. These colonies were divided up into **regions**. They were named like this:

NEW ENGLAND: Massachusetts, New Hampshire, Rhode Island, Connecticut.

MID-ATLANTIC: New York, New Jersey, Pennsylvania, Delaware.

SOUTHERN: Maryland, Virginia, Georgia, North Carolina, South Carolina.

Don't see your state represented here? That's okay because later you will learn how more and more land was acquired (added on) and how America grew into the United States of America.

So, what motivated the people of England to leave their country and move all the way to the New World to start a new life in one of the three colonies? The people were pushed out of England and pulled to the New World for these reasons:

Mainly, the people wanted jobs, money, and land. They wanted something else, too. They wanted the freedom to worship how they wanted. In England, the people were told how to worship - Catholic. Some people did not want to be told how to worship, so moving to a new country sounded like a good solution to that problem.

Now, let's look at a map of what the original 13 colonies looked like. When you look at this map, ask yourself these questions:

- What region would you want to live in? Why?
- What do you know about the states that were in the first 13 colonies? Explain.
- If you had to guess, what types of jobs do you think were available in each of the regions? Why do you think that?
- Do you see the rest of America on the map? Who do you think lived in those areas? Write them down.

Figure 2

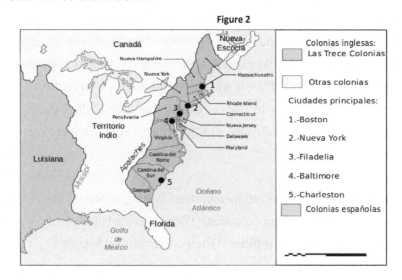

Questions:

1.   Why did England want to settle land in The New World?

2.   What motivated the people of England to move to America, or "The New World?"

3.   What are the names of the 3 regions of America during this time?

4.   How do you think the people traveled to The New World from England? Explain.

5.   What do you predict will happen when the people arrive in their new land?

WRITE!

Imagine that you are living in England, and that you want to move to the New World. Make a list of all the reasons you might want to leave your country and travel to an unknown place.

Now, write a letter to your friend/husband/wife/children explaining why you want to go on this adventure. Don't forget to include things you are afraid of, things you are excited about, and what you would like to do when you arrive.

Lesson 1.2: The Regions and What They Represented

Did you guess that the people of England had to travel by sea to arrive in The New World? Good job! Many people who wanted to live there left everything they knew behind in England to start fresh in a new land. Some people did not have any money to pay for the trip in order to take them to The New World. These people traded future work for their passage. They were called **The Virginia Company.** Many rich landowners needed help with their farms, so they paid for the passage of people from England who wanted to come to in exchange for free work on their farm. Some people were never able to fully pay off their debt and were servants forever. This is referred to as *indentured servitude,* or **indentured servants.**

Each region had something different to offer. Let's start with New England.

NEW ENGLAND: This region was very similar to England. They were mostly Catholic. The religious leaders made the rules and laws of this region. This is called **egalitarian**. Their laws came from England - these laws were called **The Magna Carta**. They voted using a **popular government** system, which means the most popular vote won. They had **town meetings** and met at **parliament**, which is the actual building where they made the laws.

The people in this region were called **Puritans** and **Pilgrims**. They were very, very religious people. They believed that if someone did not worship the way they did, they should not live there. How did they make money? In this region, **shipbuilding, fishing, and commerce** were the main jobs. Because the colonies in this region were located right on the ocean, these jobs were the best suited for this area. Also, it gets really cold for many months of the year in this area, so farming was not a good fit because of this.

MID-ATLANTIC: This region was accepting of any religion, as long as it was Christian. They were called **Quakers**. Most of the people who settled here were Catholics. They mainly grew **staple crops** such as wheat and corn.

SOUTHERN: This region was full of landowners. The colonies in this region had good, warm weather almost year-round, so farming **tobacco, indigo, and rice** were the main jobs here. In the southern region, the landowners made the laws. This is called a **hierarchical** government. The landowners used **slaves** to work the farms. They did not pay the slaves for their work, so they made lots and lots of money. Remember, money and power go together! In the southern region, the landowners were called **Aristocrats**. The landowners represented the government. The **House of Burgess** was an example of a representative government in the southern region. In this form of government, they would elect one person to represent the people's vote. The landowners had large **plantations** of farmland and they did not care what religion a person was. They only cared about money and making more and more of it!

Now that you know a little more about each region, answer the following questions:

- Where would you want to live if you moved from England to America during this time? Why? Explain your answer.
- Which region was most like England? Why do you think they would want to be set up almost exactly like England, but in America? Explain.
- What is the difference between an indentured servant and a slave? Explain.
- Look at the picture below. These two people were early settlers in America. Their names were ROGER WILLIAMS and ANNE HUTCHISON. They were kicked out of their region because of their religious beliefs. Where do you think they originally settled? Why do you think so?

Anne Hutchison and Roger Williams being exiled from one region due to their religious beliefs.

Figure 3

NOTES:

Lesson 1.3: The Colonists: Independent or Not?

The people in the colonies, **the colonists**, found different ways to make money in their new land. Because England owned the land, the colonists sent small portions of the money they made back to England ("the mother country"). Have you heard of **taxes**? This is what they did. They paid taxes to England on everything they made. They also sent goods back to England for them to use. This is called **mercantilism.**

Many of the colonists found new ways to make extra money by traveling out into the Atlantic Ocean and the Caribbean Sea by boat. They started to trade things that they had for things the other countries had. When they did this, they would bring the new things back to America and keep them for themselves. They would not send money in the form of taxes back to England for these things. Some examples of what they were getting were *sugar, rum, and slaves.*

The trade route looked like a triangle shape in the ocean. It was called the Triangle Trade or the Atlantic World. Here is a picture of what it looked like:

Figure 4

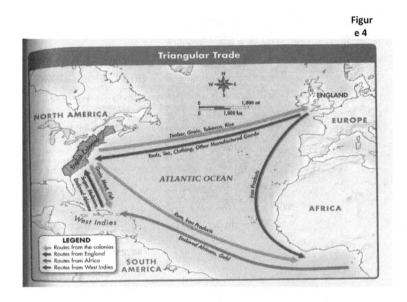

England currently had so much money, they didn't really watch the colonists and what they were doing. This "not watching" is called **Salutary Neglect**. They didn't really know that the colonists were making money through the triangle trade because they were not watching them closely. As a result, the colonists were getting rich.

Once they finally started to notice, suddenly they wanted more taxes and more money from the colonists. England started to abuse the colonists in different ways. These abuses are called

usurpations. Basically, they tried to take their power away from them, and the colonists became very angry at the **King of England, King George**, for suddenly wanting to control them after years of not watching or caring what they did.

One thing that happened was that he told the colonists NOT to cross over from their colonies to the land next to them that was owned by France. There was an imaginary line that divided the colonies, owned by England, and the other land owned by France. This line was called **The Proclamation Line**.

The colonists crossed over that line and started stealing things from the French, like furs. The French of course got angry, and a war started between the people that lived on the French side (Indians), and the colonists. This war was called **The French and Indian War** and it was from 1754-1763. (Almost 10 years of fighting!)

Here is what the Proclamation Line looked like: It is in red.

Figure 5

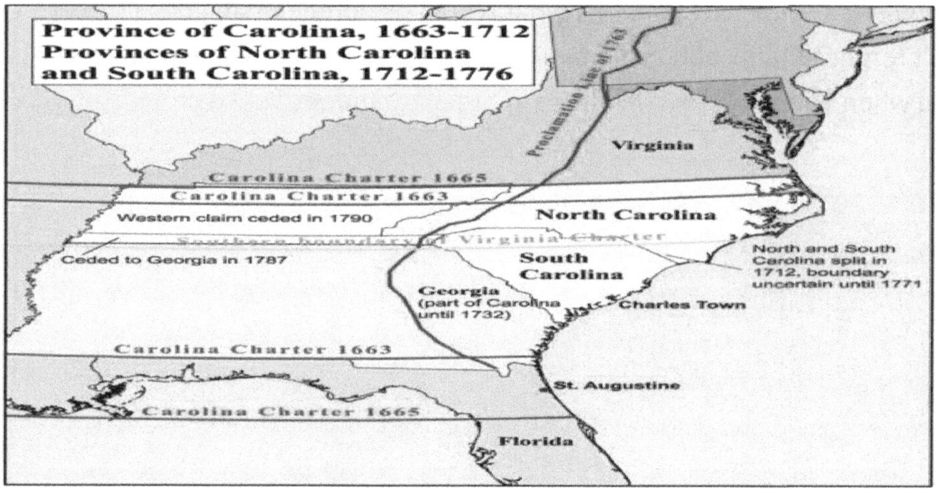

See if you can answer these questions:

1. How did the colonists make even more money than they were already making? Explain.

2. What is salutary neglect? Give an example of how England did this to the colonists.

3. How did England make money from the colonists? Explain.

4. What was the proclamation line?

5. How did the French and Indian War start? Explain.

WRITE!

Think of ways that people make money in your world today. Do people in your life have only one job? Do they do anything else to make extra money? Make a list of ways that people can make extra money.

Now, write a plan for what job you would like to have in the future. If you were able to have this job and needed some extra money, what would be some possibilities for you to earn it? Don't forget to think about the typical working hours that you would have in your job and when you would be able to earn the extra money.

Lesson 1.4: After the French & Indian War

War costs a lot of money. England supplied guns, ammo, etc. to the colonists to fight the war against the French. When the war was over, England wanted their money back! They decided to tax the colonists to get their money back. How did they do this? They taxed them on **Sugar (The Sugar Act, 1764)**. They taxed them on **Stamps (The Stamp Act, 1765).** They taxed them on many other things that they used on a regular basis like paint, lead, and paper. These taxes were named **The Townshend Acts, 1767.**

The colonists were very angry with England for taxing them on all of these things when they never cared about them before. They started to shout, **"No taxation without representation!"** This means that they were angry that England had never represented them before, so they shouldn't get their money now.

A lot of stress started to happen in America after this.   When the tax collectors from England started to come around to America to get their money, fights broke out. The colonists even tried to hurt England by completely stopping themselves from buying anything that was made in England.

With all this stress between the colonists and England, some fights were happening, which were small. However, some of the news was spreading lies that the fighting was much bigger. This "fake news" is called **yellow journalism.** One of the most famous "fake news" stories during this time was called **The Boston Massacre.** Some colonists in Boston, Massachusetts had a small fight with some people who were there from England. The newspapers spread a story that guns and ammo were being used and many people were killed on the streets in a "massacre". This fake news only made the stress worse and made people want to fight even more.

NOTES:

The Boston Massacre

Figure 6

England started to realize that the stress was getting bad, so they decided to stop asking for tax money from the colonists on everything except for one thing: tea. They really did not want to fight the colonists. The colonists reacted to this by getting on a ship in Massachusetts and throwing all the tea overboard into the water. They said, "we don't want your tea." This was called **The Boston Tea Party** and it happened in 1773. (The late 18th century)

Figure 7

When this happened, England sent all their troops over to America to try to get things under control. The colonists responded by training troops to be prepared to fight at any moment. These troops were called **Minutemen.** Well, in 1775 the very first fight broke out between the colonists and England. It was called **Lexington and Concord.** Now the colonists decided to write a break-up letter to King George. They wanted their independence. This letter was called **The Declaration of Independence.** The colonists were now at war with England. This was called **The Revolutionary War.**

See if you can answer these questions:

1. How did England try to get their money back from the French and Indian War?

2. Explain, "no taxation without representation!" What does it mean?

3. What was the Declaration of Independence?

4. Why was the Boston Massacre an example of yellow journalism? Explain.

5. Why did the colonists throw out all the tea? Explain.

WRITE!

Think about ways that the media today can shape your opinion or the opinions of others. Make a list of things you think of. Next, think about if the media has influence over the people. Don't forget to include all types of media such as newspapers, social media, and television.

Now, write to explain a time when you or someone in your life was influenced by the media and what happened as a result. Include your opinion on if the media was "fake news" or reporting the truth.

Lesson 1.5: Colonists Win the Revolutionary War! Time to Write America's Laws

The colonists won the Revolutionary War and now they had their independence from England, thanks to the help from the French. In 1776 the colonists wrote **The Articles of Confederation**. This was a set of rules or laws that America would follow. There were problems, though, with the Articles of Confederation. Here are some of them:

- Each state had its own rules, so they were like their own, separate, countries.
- Each state had its own money and its own taxes.
- There was no President. There were no courts.
- It was a weak system of government.

One thing that happened that showed how weak the government was involved a farmer in Massachusetts named **Daniel Shay.** He was having a bad year and could not pay his bills. The state of Maryland came after him and tried to take his land away from him. Daniel got angry at the state and went to all the other farmers he knew and told them, "If this can happen to me, it can happen to you." They all got together and started to fight against the state. This was called **Shay's Rebellion**.

The other states heard about it and did not want to get involved because they had their own state to worry about. This was the first thing that happened that showed that the states should really come together as one to become stronger.

Figure 8

Shay's Rebellion

A big meeting was planned in Philadelphia to work on how to come together as one nation. This meeting was called **The Constitutional Convention.** It happened in the summer of 1787.

Many important leaders were there to fix the problems with the Articles of Confederation, and they actually ended up writing a whole new document. This was called **The United States Constitution**, and it is the law still used today in America. Here are some things that were written:

- The state taxes still happened, but now the United States also taxed the people.
- The **HOUSE** and the **SENATE** was formed.
- **Interstate Commerce** was formed which meant the people could buy/sell/trade with other states.
- There was one **currency** (money).
- No more **rebellions** (like with Daniel Shay), within the states.

Information about the HOUSE:
- They are elected members that represent each state. They are elected by the people in that state to represent what the people want. (**direct popular vote**)
- Some states have more representatives than others because this is determined by the state's population.

Information about the SENATE:
- Each state has two senators.
- The senators are elected by the people of that state. (This came later with the Populist party, which you will learn about soon).

America follows this two-house system, which is known as a **bi-cameral legislation.**

Questions

1. What were the first laws/rules of America called?
2. What was the biggest problem with the first laws in America?

3. Why did the leaders need to meet after Shay's Rebellion.

4. What is bi-cameral legislation?

Lesson 1.6: Congress, The Electoral College, & The Bill of Rights

One of the terms you need to understand before we move forward is **Congress.** What is that, exactly? This refers to all the elected representatives for each state. All the representatives (from the HOUSE and from the SENATE) meet as one in Washington, D.C. to vote on certain issues/laws that have to do with the **federal government**. Remember: the federal government refers to the entire United States of America - all the states together. Congress meets in the Capitol building in Washington, D.C. to vote on things for the federal government. Ok, back to the Constitutional Convention.......

Figure 9

NOTES:

Many compromises were made in order to write the Constitution. This means the people gave up some of what they wanted for some of the things others wanted so that an agreement could be reached. Here are some of the different plans that were agreed upon at the Constitutional Convention.

The Virginia Plan: This plan wanted a **bi-cameral legislature** (2 houses of congress) The **House of Representatives** was one and the **Senate** was the other.

This is how it works: For a new law to become a real law it first has to be presented to the **House of Representatives**. If it passes here, then it goes to the **Senate**. If it passes the Senate, it becomes a new law. (Remember….this is for each state)

The New Jersey Plan: This plan was completely the opposite of the Virginia Plan. It wanted an equal representation from each state to make up Congress. No bi-cameral legislature.

The Great Compromise: The leaders took a little from the Virginia Plan and a little from The New Jersey Plan and compromised. (You will learn more about this later)

There was one more thing called the Three Fifths Compromise. This one said that a slave only counted as ⅗ of a person to represent Congress in America. Why is this important? Because the number of House of Representatives that each state has is based on that state's population. So, a slave did not count as a whole person.

America also needed a President. To elect a President, the people came up with a system called **The Electoral College**. This system works by allowing each state to send **electors** to cast votes for President. Each state has a certain number of electors. Once a candidate for President gets 270 votes then they win the Presidency. What does this mean? This means that the popular vote from the actual people who live in America does influence the electors, but the electors are the ones who actually determine the Presidency. Because some states have more people than others, they are only given a limited number of electoral votes to keep it fair. In short: the popular vote doesn't necessarily determine the Presidency, the electoral vote does.

Let's break down the electoral college:

Each state gets a certain number of electors (a person that represents the people).The number of electors is based on the population of the state.

- The elector is usually someone that is already involved in some type of politics.
- Each elector takes the votes of the people from the state and is supposed to cast a vote at Congress for the President. This is called an electoral vote.
- There is a total of 538 electoral votes in the entire United States.
- The person that gets more than half of the electoral votes wins the Presidency.

Okay, now that the people had a compromise on the new law (The Constitution), America still had to vote on adopting it. They needed 9 states to **ratify** (this word means vote) on the Constitution for it to be passed. At this time, there were two groups with different belief systems in America and they were named **The Federalists** and **The Anti-Federalists.** Here is what they believed:

THE FEDERALISTS

They wanted a strong central government

They wanted a better economy.

They wanted law and order.

THE ANTI-FEDERALISTS

They wanted less National government: They wanted the States to have the power.

They wanted unlimited terms.

They wanted a list of people's rights. (**Bill of Rights**)

Some of the leaders of the Federalist belief were **James Madison, Alexander Hamilton,** and **John Jay.** They wrote **The Federalist Papers**, which tried to persuade people to love the new Constitution. The Anti-Federalists did not like the Constitution like it was. They wanted there to be a **Bill of Rights** to protect the people. The first 10 **amendments** (changes) to the Constitution were called the **Bill of Rights**. As you can see, the Constitution was a compromise between what the Federalists wanted and what the Anti-Federalists wanted.

 **The United States Constitution was written.**

Figure 10

Questions:

1. What is Congress?

2. How does a state pass a law? What is the process?

3. What important document was written at the Constitutional Convention?

4. What is the Bill of Rights?
5. How is a President elected in America? (electoral college) Explain.

WRITE!

Think about what you have learned about how laws get passed in America. On a piece of paper, draw a chart, visual representation, or pictures to show the steps necessary for a law to be passed in America.

Show your project to a friend or family member and explain the steps!

Lesson 1.7: The Branches of Government and The First President

In America, the people have what is called **The Rule of Law**. This means that every person is under the law, including the Congressmen, the President, the Judges, everybody. A **Constitutional Government** is a **Limited Government**. Americans have **Federalism** which is a shared power between the national government and the state government. A good example of this is that in the states there is a city police department and a state police department. They have a shared responsibility to govern the people in the state.

The Constitution says that the people have certain freedoms. This means that the national government protects a person's freedoms, and the state governments cannot violate that. The powers are broken down like this:

Delegated Powers: Powers given to the federal government (national government).
Reserved Powers: Powers kept by the states and the people.
Concurrent Powers: These are shared between the national and the state governments.

There are also different branches of our government. Here they are:

Legislative: They make the laws.
Executive: They enforce the laws.
Judicial: They judge the person who breaks the laws.

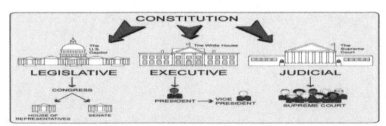

Figure 11

This separation of powers is called an **Ordered Government**.

America's first President was **George Washington**. He needed people to help him run the country. These people were called his **cabinet.** He chose **Thomas Jefferson, Alexander Hamilton, Henry Knox,** and **Edmund Randolph**. Guess what? Thomas Jefferson and Alexander Hamilton did not agree on how things should be run in the country, and they fought constantly.

This was the start of our **party system** that exists today, the **democrats** and the **republicans.** They fought a lot over disagreements on how to run the country. Some had good ideas, and some did not have good ideas, and they fought about it. Some thought America should have a Laissez-Faire government - one in which the government did not get involved with what people did with their money. Others felt the government should be more involved. Fighting, arguing, and more fighting happened.

Alexander Hamilton came up with an idea on how to handle the nation's debt:

Have **public credit** (a system of borrowing money)
Have a **National Bank**
All products should be made in America. (**domestic manufacturing**)

Alexander Hamilton thought money could be loaned to other countries, **interest** could be collected (money) from them when they paid back their loans, and then that interest could be used to pay back debts owed. This was called **Hamiltonian Economics.**

Well, **George Washington** hated this plan.   He also saw his two friends fighting every day in the office and he said that *America could not survive if it had political parties and alliances with foreign countries.*

Finally, George Washington quit. Now there was a new election for President. The enemies who fought constantly were running against each other for the Presidency. **The Election of 1796** was John Adams v. Thomas Jefferson.

In those times, the person who lost became the **Vice President.** John Adams won, so Thomas Jefferson became the Vice President. So, now two men who did not agree on anything were running the country together! They could not agree, so one went to the northern part of America and the other one went to the southern part. This divided the country. This is called **Sectionalism.**

They talked a lot of trash about each other, and they also wrote laws to try to stop each other from getting anything done. John Adams wrote a law that said Thomas Jefferson could not talk trash about him anymore. This was called **The Alien and Sedition Acts of 1798** and it also said that America needed to limit the activities of all illegal immigrants in the country.

Thomas Jefferson said, "you can't do this!". He got together with his friend James Madison and they wrote **The Virginia and Kentucky Resolutions** which said the people of Virginia and Kentucky (the states where they lived) don't have to follow the national law. People can say anything whenever they want to thanks to **The Bill of Rights.**

Questions:

1. Which branch of our government would be in charge of punishing someone for committing a crime?

2. Which branch of our government would determine the consequence of someone who broke the law?

3. What did Alexander Hamilton and Thomas Jefferson fight about the most?

4. What did George Washington say would break up our country?

5. Explain sectionalism.

6. What were the Alien and Sedition Acts of 1798?

WRITE!

Think about what George Washington said would break up America. Now, write to explain if you agree or disagree with him on this issue. Give reasons for your opinion.

Lesson 1.8: The Revolution of 1800

The Revolution of 1800 was not an actual physical fight. It was the election of 1800 where Thomas Jefferson defeated John Adams for the Presidency. The Federalists were very unhappy with the result of this election because their belief system was totally different from Thomas Jefferson's. Also, Thomas Jefferson said that he would destroy Federalism. The Federalists were getting together and trying to figure out a way to stop this from happening. They came up with a plan, too.

First, did you know that when a President gets elected in November that the job doesn't actually start for 4 months! From November until January in a new Presidency, this is called the **Lame Duck Session**. The former President is still in control of the country until January. So, this means that after a new President is elected in November, the old administration still has control and can make changes to the government for 4 months until the new President takes over.

Figure 12

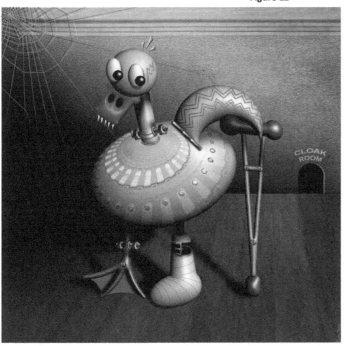

Now that you know what the lame duck session is, here is what happened. During the lame duck session after Thomas Jefferson was elected President, the Federalists decided that they would appoint Federalist Judges in the one court that ruled over all the other smaller courts in the nation: **The Supreme Court.**

If the Judge has the final decision in court cases and that Judge is a Federalist, they would be able to keep Federalist policies in place.   So, they created 16 new courts and appointed Federalist Judges to all 16 of these courts. What this did was every time the President, Thomas Jefferson, tried to pass anything through the highest court, the Federalist Judge would not allow it. These Federalist Judges were known as **The Midnight Judges.** Why this name? Because this was something that happened at "the last minute" of one President being in power and another one taking over. (during the lame duck period)

Questions:

1.   What was the Revolution of 1800?

2.   What did Thomas Jefferson say he would do as President?

3.   What is the lame duck session?

4.   How did the Federalists use the lame duck session to keep their belief system in place?

5.   What was a Midnight Judge?

6.   What is the highest court in the nation called?

7.   Do you think the Federalists had a good plan to keep their belief system in place? Why or why not?

PROJECT!

On a piece of paper, draw a large picture of a duck to represent the lame duck session you have learned about. On the back of the duck write some points to remember about the lame duck session to help you remember. Cut the duck out and color it. Place it in your journal or notes for Standard 1 to refer to later.

Lesson 1.9: Important Court Cases

As you've learned, The Supreme Court is the highest court in the land. The Supreme Court makes the final decision on laws, not the President and not Congress. In this country, important cases that were brought before this court are studied and referred to for future issues. Here are some of the most important cases that went before The Supreme Court in the early years of America.

Marbury v Madison: The Supreme Court can decide if something is constitutional or unconstitutional. The power of Judicial Review.

McCullough v Maryland: This case ruled that states cannot tax the federal government.

Gibbons v Ogden: This case ruled that the federal government controls all the trade between the states.

Figure 13

The Supreme Court decides whether we keep a law or not. They decide if a law is Constitutional or Unconstitutional (lawful or not lawful). This process of making these decisions is called **Judicial Review**. Also, once a Supreme Court Judge is appointed to his or her position, they stay there for life. All previously ruled cases are examined in determining future cases.

Lesson 1.9 (A): Growing America and Another War

Thomas Jefferson was the President of the United States at this point in history. It was the early 1800's - known as the 19th century. As a nation, the people were very proud of what they had accomplished. They were proud to be Americans, and this is called **Nationalism**. They were getting very rich and powerful during this time. So, now they really wanted to explore and grow. They wanted more and more land to get bigger.

Thomas Jefferson bought a huge amount of land from the leader of France. His name was **Napoleon Bonaparte**. It was so much land, and it doubled the size of America! It was called **The Louisiana Purchase.**

Figure 14

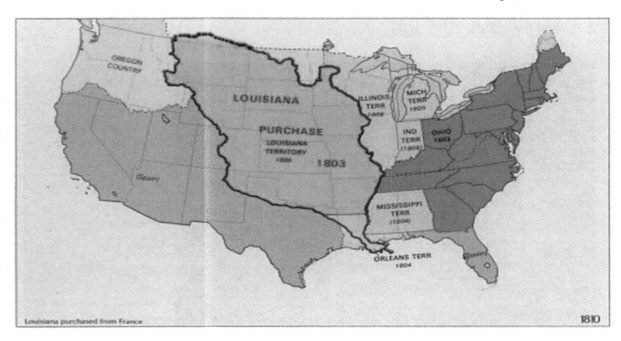

Next, Thomas Jefferson got together with the famous explorers **Lewis and Clark** and he sent them out to find and map the land. Thomas Jefferson believed in a **Laissez Faire** method, which meant that he believed in trading and doing business with everybody, every nation.

Something happened when America tried to trade with England. They took supplies and forced the people to join the British Navy. This was called **impressing**. They were still very angry with America about winning the Revolutionary War. To solve the problem of **impressing**, America tried to stop trading with them. This is called **embargo**. America created the **Embargo Act of 1807** which said they would not trade with England anymore. They wanted to try to hurt them financially, but they did not want to go to war with them, because war was expensive and they were buying so much land at that time, they did not need more debt.

While this was happening, NEW ENGLAND really hated this plan because their whole way of life was based on shipbuilding and trade with other countries, such as England. They were not happy with Thomas Jefferson because this decision was really hurting their economy (which means it was costing them money). There were certain people in America that hated the embargo against England. They made fun of the government by creating cartoon drawings for the newspaper so others could see and make fun of the government, too. There were a couple of guys who were called **Warhawks** that were tough guys that wanted to go to war with England because of the **impressing** they were doing. Their names were **Henry Clay (from Kentucky)** and **John C. Calhoun (from South Carolina)**.

Figure 15

A political cartoon for the OGRABME policy.

A new President was elected around this time, and his name was **James Madison.** Madison agreed with the Warhawks and decided to go to war with England again. This was called **The War of 1812**. Well, this war didn't go so well for America. Their military wasn't very strong at the time and England was winning every battle in the beginning. Finally, out of nowhere there was a battle in the city of New Orleans (that is in Louisiana). **Andrew Jackson** was a leader in the military there and he won this battle known as **The Battle of New Orleans**. The people were so happy to win, they made him a national hero. Today there is a beautiful park named after Andrew Jackson in New Orleans called Jackson Square.

Jackson became like an overnight hero. He started to just give away land to the average, common white man (white man meaning NOT the Native Americans). He basically kicked the Native Americans off their land and gave the land to common white men who wouldn't normally be able to afford it. This made him very, very popular. Have you guessed yet? If you were a landowner back in that time, that means that you had the power to vote. This became known as **Jacksonian Democracy** and he hooked his friends up with jobs in the government. This is known as **the spoils system.** Maybe Andrew Jackson wanted their vote for later on.....what do you think?

It's really sad what happened to the Native Americans during this time. They were being kicked off their land. America sent tribes like the **Seminoles** and the **Cherokees** off their land and sent them to a new area called Oklahoma. This was called **The Trail of Tears** because as the Native Americans left their homeland they cried along the trail to Oklahoma.

Figure 16

R. Michelson Galleries   "The Trail of Tears"   © Max D. Standley

Questions:

1. What is an embargo?

2. What does laissez faire mean?

3. What was England doing when we tried to trade with them?

4. Who were the Warhawks?

5. How did Andrew Jackson become a hero?

6. What did Andrew Jackson begin to do after becoming a hero?

7. What happened to the Native Americans as America grew?

WRITE!

Imagine that you were a Native American living during this time period. Write a letter to your cousin who lives in another part of the country to explain what is happening to you and your family. Don't forget to include your emotions and feelings about everything

UNIT 2: EXPANSION and UNION
Lesson 2.1: Manifest Destiny

Let's take a quick look back to Unit 1 when England first sent people over to America to settle the land. Well, you know what? England was not the only country doing that at the time. Spain and Portugal - they were also taking land in America and settling it. That is one reason why we have so many different languages in America now. Well, the President during this time was **James Monroe**. He did not like the European countries settling any more land in America. He came up with the **Monroe Doctrine** (a doctrine is a belief or set of beliefs).   This doctrine said that no other countries could settle any more of American land.

So, at the very same time, there was a belief that was sweeping over America called **manifest destiny**. This belief was that it was the destiny of Americans to move west and acquire more and more land. It was deeply believed that the angels of heaven wanted Americans to move west and expand their territory. There were even pictures of the angel guiding people to go west. Even though the Native Americans were being kicked off their land, the people believed that it was their destiny to do this. Here is a good picture:

Figure 17

So, people were moving west and excited about what they would do when they got there. They hoped for gold, money, better farming, and new inventions for a better life. Something that was always asked, though, when Americans conquered new lands was this, **"do we have slaves here, or not?"** America always wanted to keep a balance of slave states and non-slave states. Mainly in the northern areas of America, there were no slaves.

But in the southern areas, there were slaves to work on the plantations. So, as the people headed west, the question always came up.....**"do we have slaves here, or not?"** Remember: America wanted to keep that balanced.

Questions:

1.   What was the Monroe Doctrine?

2.   What was Manifest Destiny?

3.   Why do you think America wanted to keep a balance between slave states and non- slave states? Explain.

PROJECT!

On a poster, draw a map of America. Next, draw small pictures labeling the movement to the West and all the progress that went with that. Include things like horses, wagons, railroad tracks that were being built, Native Americans, bison, etc. Don't forget the picture representation of the angel for Manifest Destiny!

Lesson 2.2:   Trouble in Texas

Let's talk about Texas. Remember, back in the 1800's, when America was moving west and acquiring more and more land, Texas was owned by Mexico. As Americans headed west, Mexico told them they could come into Texas territory and stay, but that they could not bring any slaves into the area! Well, the Americans brought the slaves with them anyway. This made Mexico very, very angry. The Mexicans were kicking out the Americans because they broke the rules.

There was a famous battle where the Mexicans came into San Antonio (a city in Texas) where there were a lot of Americans that had settled and brought slaves. They went in and killed every single man, woman, and child there to show the Americans, "this is what happens when you break our rules!" This battle was called **The Battle of the Alamo**, and it happened in 1836.

The Battle of the Alamo Figure 18

Another battle came shortly thereafter where the people who lived in Texas fought back against the Mexican government for what happened at The Alamo. This was called **The Battle of San Jacinto**. In this battle, Mexico said, "we don't want you anymore, Texas!" So, Texas became independent from Mexico. They were not a part of Mexico anymore, and they were also not a part of America. They became their very own country, known as **The Lone Star State.**

Figure 19

America was kind of interested in taking Texas, but they didn't want to battle with Mexico, so they left Texas alone. Texas became known as **The Republic of Texas**. This happened in 1837, just one year after the Battle of the Alamo. Texas had their own money, their own laws, and everything. They were very big, and they were their own, independent country!

Questions:

1. What did Mexico say to Americans if they came to Texas?

2. When the Americans did not follow the rules, what happened?

3. What battle gave Texas their independence from Mexico?
4. Why did America not want Texas at this time?

Lesson 2.3: The Mexican Cession

In 1844 America had a new President. His name was **James Polk**. Guess what? Polk really wanted Texas! He was not afraid to go to war with Mexico if Mexico decided they didn't want America to have Texas. He knew that the people that lived in Texas already figured out how to fight against the Mexicans because they had been in battles with them before. He got together with Texas and made an agreement to **annex** them into America (this means to make them a part of America).

When this happened, a war started between Mexico and America called **The Mexican War.** America marched right into Mexico City and basically took over the city. Troops took over the hotels, the restaurants, everything. They occupied the whole city. Mexico hated this. They loved Mexico City and they got very tired of the Americans being there taking over everything. So, this is the incredible thing that happened next:

Mexico got together with America and agreed to a **treaty** (an agreement). They agreed to give America a huge, huge piece of land that they owned at that time. This land was called **The Mexican Cession**. This land included the states of California, Nevada, Utah, and Arizona. America agreed to take this land as their own and to move out of Mexico City in exchange for this. This treaty was called **The Treaty of Guadalupe Hidalgo** and it made America so huge. This is part of the reason that so many people speak Spanish in those states today because those states were once owned by Mexico.

Figure 20

Just after this America also got the state of Oregon from Britain. They did not go to war for this, they just reached an agreement and got it in **The Oregon Treaty**. This is how America got so huge.

Questions:

1. Why did Mexico give America so much land? Explain.

2. What is a treaty?

WRITE!

In your journal, write your opinion about if you think James Polk was a good President. Explain with details showing what you've learned about his Presidency.

Lesson 2.4:   America Becomes Divided

Well, all this land America got was definitely making them more powerful, but because some states had slaves and others did not, the country started to become divided in their beliefs. This made the people begin to argue. After the Mexican Cession land the balance of slave states to no slave states became a problem because that was a lot of land. Basically, the northern part of the United States was against slavery. The southern part of the United States was in favor of slavery. The main reason for this was that in the south there were large plantations that relied on slaves to work the land to be able to make big money. The north did not have large plantations.

When America got the Mexican Cession land it became divided into 3 sections which were the north, the south, and the west. This is called **sectionalism.** Each section had powerful political leaders. They were **Henry Clay** for the west, **John C. Calhoun** for the south, and **Daniel Webster** for the north. To try to better balance the slave states with the non-slave states, America had something called **The Missouri Compromise**, which happened in 1820. This is what divided the nation into the three sections. There was an imaginary line drawn right down the center of the country. To the north of the line was considered no slaves and to the south was considered slave states.

Figure 21

The Missouri Compromise

Each section depended on different things to live. The north depended on **industry, commerce, trading, factories, shipbuilding**. The west depended on the **railroad and farming**.

The south depended on **farming**. Henry Clay in the west did not like trading with other countries. He wanted us to use the railroad system to trade only within the United States. He wanted America to be a self-sufficient country. Daniel Webster in the north agreed with this. He also did not want to trade with other countries. But the south - they wanted to trade with other countries.

These differences in opinions about slavery and trade created stress and tension for the people. Soon, America would go to war over these disagreements. This war was between the north and the south. This was called the **Civil War.** The period of time before this war was called **The Antebellum Period.**

There were other problems besides the balance of slaves and non-slaves and trading with other countries. Here are some of the problems in the **Antebellum Period.**

ABOLITIONISM: Someone named **William Lloyd Garrison** had a newspaper and he wrote about how cruel it was to have slaves. People started to read it and agree with him. They started to become angry.

WOMEN'S RIGHTS: People started to say, "well if slaves should be free and equal, so should women." A woman named **Elizabeth Cady Stanton** was important during this time in stating that women should have the right to vote!

TEMPERANCE MOVEMENT: This was another issue. It had to do with drinking alcohol. Some people believed that Americans should not drink alcohol at all, ever. They believed if they had manifest destiny and were being led by God and the angels, surely, they do not want the people drinking.

THE SECOND GREAT AWAKENING: This was about religion. Baptists and Methodists started becoming very popular during this time. This really got people thinking about how the slaves were being treated in this country. Surely this was not right.

As you can see, all these **social issues** got people more and more involved in what was happening with slavery and the treatment of people, and whether it was right or wrong. This helped to fuel the motivation for the **Civil War.**

Questions:

1. What was the purpose of the Missouri Compromise?

2. What were the three sections of the United States and what did they believe?

3. Why do you think that the South wanted to trade with foreign countries?

4. Why did the social issues of the Antebellum period lead to a Civil War? Explain.

Lesson 2.5: Antebellum Period

Henry Clay, who represented the western part of America supported an idea called **The American System** which meant the people would have:

A National Bank
Internal improvements (ex: linking the West to ports and factories in the North by building railroads and canals so it would be possible to trade within America)
Protective Tariff - no trading with other countries. If trading with other countries a very high tax must be paid.

Henry Clay - Known as "The Great Compromiser"

Figure 22

Andrew Jackson was the President that incorporated the protective tariff into law in America, but South Carolina and other states in the South really hated this idea. Why? Because they were farmers and they wanted to be able to continue to trade with Europe and other foreign countries. This is how they made most of their money. So, South Carolina's John C. Calhoun decided to **nullify** the protective tariff. This means they won't pay, and they won't follow the rule. They called it the **Tariff of Abomination**. They said this law was unconstitutional so they would not pay it. This was known as the **Nullification Crisis,** and it went on for a period of about 5 years (1828-1833).

Since the protective tariff was Henry Clay's idea, he wanted to try to make everyone happy in this situation. He was known as **The Great Compromiser**. Remember, the people in the South were really angry about this tariff because it was seriously hurting their economy. They also wanted to keep their slaves because that helped them to make more money. Not everyone in the United States agreed that having slaves was a good thing, so they were arguing about that. There was talk from a man up North named David Wilmot that all the new land from Mexico (Mexican Cession) should have no slaves. He tried to get this law passed, but it did not pass. **(Wilmot Proviso)** But just the thought of something like this happening really upset the Southern states and great fighting occurred over this idea.

About the slavery issue: there were a couple of different opinions. There was a group called **Abolitionists** and they were totally against slavery. Then there was another group of people called **Free Soilers** who believed in slavery as long as they were not going into the new territories America had just gained. Basically, the Free Soilers did not want slavery to spread. The reason for this was that they believed the slaves could take away jobs by working on the land that was new to the United States.

Here's where Henry Clay comes in to try to make everyone happy in **The Compromise of 1850.**

California would be a free state (no slaves)
Stronger fugitive slave laws (this means if slaves tried to escape, they would be punished and returned to their owners)
Popular Sovereignty (this means that the people in the Mexican Cession states got to vote on if they would have slaves and the most popular vote would win)
Texas would sell some land to the Federal Government and take all their debts from their war. In the city of **Washington**, there would be no slaves at all.

NOTES:

Questions:

1. What was meant by internal improvements? Explain.

2. What was the protective tariff?

3. Why did the Southern states hate the protective tariff? Explain.

4. Who nullified the protective tariff?
5. What was the nickname of the protective tariff?
6. How long did the Nullification Crisis go on?
7. How did David Wilmot try to stop slavery? Explain.

8. What is the difference between an abolitionist and a Free Soiler?

9. What is a fugitive slave law?

10. What is popular sovereignty?

WRITE!

In your journal, make a list of pros and cons. Imagine that you are a slave. List the pros and cons for you with the Compromise of 1850. Now do the same for an American in the South. What about an American in the North? How about pros and cons if you were a business owner in the North or in the South? What about if you were living in the new territory in the West?

Lesson 2.6: Lots of Disagreement in the United States

Henry Clay tried so hard to keep the country from fighting, but things were still getting tense among the people - especially when it came to the issue of slavery. **William Lloyd Garrison** was a popular writer at this time, and he wrote **The Liberator**, which was a newspaper about abolishing slavery.

In the North, there was something called the **Personal Liberty Laws** that said if a slave escaped to the state of Wisconsin, he would not be sent back. Of course, this went against the Compromise of 1850, which was a national law.

There was another popular writer named **Harriett Beecher Stowe**. She wrote a book about how bad slavery was. It was called **Uncle Tom's Cabin**. It showed pictures of slaves being beaten by their owners, and it told the truth about the treatment of the slaves in the South.

Then there was the **Kansas-Nebraska Act** which gave Kansas and Nebraska the ability to vote on slavery. (Called **Popular Sovereignty**). Then the Free Soilers started their own party called **The Republican Party.** This was in the year 1854. Meanwhile in Kansas and Nebraska a huge fight broke out and many people were hurt. The fighting was all about the issue of slavery and this event was called **Bleeding Kansas**.

John Brown was a violent abolitionist. He and his sons along with some other people got together and seized a federal arsenal (the place where all the guns and ammunition is kept). Military was sent in, and Brown was executed.

Another event that happened was at Congress. Preston Brooks from South Carolina beat Charles Sumner from Massachusetts with his cane! They were arguing over the issue of slavery in America. This was called the **Brooks/Sumner Incident.**

NOTES:

At the Supreme Court, **Dred Scott**, a slave, sued his owner, **Sandford,** because he was being kept as a slave, but they lived in a free territory. The Supreme Court ruled that people of African descent could not be U.S. citizens and that slaves were considered property. That means that if someone owned a slave and moved to California, and they could bring that slave with them to a free state because that slave was property. This was known as **Dred Scott v. Sandford 1857**.

Figure 23

SOUTHERN CHIVALRY — ARGUMENT versus CLUB'S.

Brooks-Sumner Incident

Finally, **Abraham Lincoln** gave a famous speech called **House Divided** in 1858. Abe Lincoln won the presidential election of 1860. When he won, some of the Southern states **seceded (**withdrew/pulled away) from America and became their own country because they did not believe in Abraham Lincoln's belief that all slaves should be free. The new Southern states called themselves the **Confederate States of America.**

Questions:

1. Explain personal liberty laws.

2. What was Uncle Tom's Cabin?

3. What was the Kansas-Nebraska Act?

41

4. Why did John Brown get executed?

5. What was Bleeding Kansas?

6. Explain the Supreme Court decision on Dred Scott v. Sandford, 1857.

7. What was the name of Abraham Lincoln's famous speech just before his election?

8. What did the Southern states do when Lincoln was elected?

9. Why did the Southern states not like Abraham Lincoln?

10. What do you think about slavery? Explain.

PROJECT!

Set up a courtroom that would be similar to the DRED SCOTT v SANDFORD case. Now, act out parts for DRED SCOTT, SANDFORD, and the JUDGE. Don't forget to think about things Dred Scott would be concerned about, as well as issues Sandford felt were of merit.

WRITE!

As an alternative to the project above, draw a dramatization of the courtroom scene for the DRED SCOTT v SANDFORD case including a key to explain what is happening and who the people involved are. Don't forget to include a short description of the case itself, as well as the outcome.

Lesson 2.7: The Civil War Begins

When the Southern states broke away from America (seceded), Abraham Lincoln was the new President. The year was 1860. Lincoln did not believe in slavery. He was from the North. **Slavery was not the only issue, though**. The Southern states relied on farming for their money and they disagreed with the tariffs concerning trade with other countries. The North did not rely on farming for their income. They relied on their factories. When the South seceded from the North this divided America. The Southern states called themselves **The Confederate States of America.** Americans were about to go to war within their own country and this is how things looked:

- The South really needed their slaves to keep up their standard of living (growing crops and making money) and they needed to be able to trade with Europe.
- The North did not rely on slaves. They had the ability to make products (in the factories) and they had lots of money and good banking. They also had the President of the United States: Abraham Lincoln. Finally, they had more people (a greater population).
- The South had better military and military leadership than the North.
- In a war situation, if the North were to invade the South, the South had "home field advantage" which means they knew the lay of the land, where everything was, the climate, etc.
- The North called themselves **The Union** and the South called themselves **The Confederates.**

The North had a plan to attack the South. This plan was called **The Anaconda Plan** and **General Winfield Scott** was the creator of this plan. In this plan they were going to surround the South with military forces, take control of the Mississippi River, take control of the coast and make it impossible for them to receive any supplies (like guns and ammunition). They were going to surround them just like a big snake, thus the name anaconda.

Figure 24

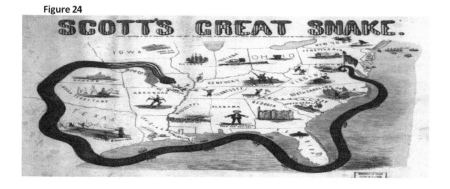

Questions:

1. What were the advantages that the North had over the South in terms of going to war?

2. What advantages did the South have over the North?

3. Why did the North not believe in slavery?

4. Besides slavery, what was the other big issue that the South had with the North? Explain.

5. Explain the picture on the previous page: The Anaconda Plan.

PROJECT!

Imagine you are General Scott speaking to his troops. Act out a scene where General Scott is explaining the anaconda plan to his troops. Include props such as a poster with pictures to show them what they will do to win the war.

Lesson 2.8: The Battles of the Civil War

Two important Generals of the Civil War were **Robert E. Lee (South)** and **Ulysses S. Grant (North)**. There was **conscription**, which is known as the **draft**. This meant that young men were forced to go to war. Back then, if a wealthy man was drafted to go to war, he could pay somebody to fight in his place and this happened often. The **anti-draft slogan** during this time was "rich man's war, poor man's fight". There were also many people that volunteered to go to war. This war was known as a **total war.** This means that there was nothing off limits. They had Generals who would rape, murder, loot-- anything and anyone in their path. **General Sherman** was famous for doing this all through the South. He burned everything in sight as he marched his troops through the South.

Figure 25

General Sherman

These are certainly not all the battles of the Civil War, but they are some of the most famous in history. The first battle of the Civil War was at **Fort Sumter** in South Carolina. It was the year 1861 and the Citadel Cadets fired the very first shots. This started the actual war. The Confederates won this battle.

The next battle was at **Antietam**. It was known as the bloodiest battle of the Civil War. Nobody actually won that battle; a lot of people died. After that, the battle of **Gettysburg** in 1863 was a turning point because the North won and continued winning battle after battle.

In **Vicksburg**, (Mississippi) the Confederates lost control of the Mississippi River. Remember the Anaconda plan? This stopped the Confederates from being able to receive any supplies for fighting the war because all the factories were in the North. By losing control of the river, they had no way to get any more supplies. **General Lee** from the South surrendered to **General Grant** at the **Appomattox Court House** in 1865 to end the Civil War.

In 1863 President Lincoln gave a famous speech called **The Emancipation Proclamation**. He said that all slaves should be free. He freed the slaves in the deep Southern states, but he kept slaves in Tennessee and Maryland because those states were between the North and the South. He kept them there to keep peace between the North and the South just after the war. Did the Emancipation Proclamation actually free the slaves? No, it did not. But it did offer them hope that someday they would be free.

Questions:

1. What is meant by "total war"? Who was most famous for this?

2. Who was the leader of the South?
3. Who was the leader of the North?
4. Who fired the first shots of the Civil War? Where was it located?

5. What was the bloodiest battle?
6. What battle allowed the North to take control of the Mississippi River?
7. Why was losing control of the river bad for the South?

8. Where did Lee surrender to Grant?
9. What was the Emancipation Proclamation?

10. What is conscription? Explain what happened.

PROJECT!

Draw a map representing the United States during the Civil War. Show each of the important battles discussed in this section. Include a key to explain any items on the map that are necessary for clarification.

Lesson 2.9: Lincoln's Plan for Reconstruction

The Civil War was over, and Abraham Lincoln had just been re-elected for another term as President of the United States. He really wanted to get things cleaned up after the war was over, but most of all he wanted the Southern states to come back to America. Everything was a big mess, and he wanted to bring the people back together and become stronger than before. He came up with an idea. The year was 1860, and he said that if 10% of the voters in the Southern states wanted to come back to the United States of America then that would be enough to bring them back. This was called **Lincoln's 10% Plan.** The only thing he wanted was for them to say they loved America and that they would free the slaves. This was called **Oath to the United States** and **Emancipate Slaves.**

But guess what happened? Before he could really get started with this process, a man named **John Wilkes Booth** came into the **Ford Theater** where Abraham Lincoln was there watching a play. He shot him and killed him (**assassination**). Booth was later hanged for this crime. With Lincoln being killed, the Vice President took over as President. His name was **Andrew Johnson.**

The period of time just after the Southern states were coming back to America was called **Presidential Reconstruction**. Here were some of the goals of Presidential Reconstruction:

- **The 13th Amendment** to the Constitution gave slaves their freedom. **TIP: easy way to remember this: slaves, unlucky, "unlucky number" 13**
- **The Freedmen's Bureau** was an agency that helped to educate African Americans by teaching them how to read, write, and how to live without being a slave.
- **Sharecropping** was introduced. This was an agreement between the landowners and the slaves. The slaves would continue living on the land and working the land, but now instead of not paying them, the landowners gave them free room and meals and they also shared the profits with them.

Andrew Johnson was not very good at keeping Presidential Reconstruction going. He was also not good at keeping the people calm. During this time something called **The Black Codes** was introduced. Even though the slaves were free, they could not go into certain stores, they could not eat with white people, and they could not go to the bathroom in the same place as white people. This was happening in the Southern states during the time of Presidential Reconstruction.

Because things were not going according to plan again in the Southern states, some Republicans from the North came up with another plan called **Congressional Reconstruction.** The Republicans in the Northern states were in power at this time because when the Southern states left America during the Civil War, all their political power left with them. With the Republican North in charge in Congress, they made all kinds of new laws that benefited the North, not the South.

The Republican North wanted to protect the African Americans. **Thaddeus Stevens** was a House Representative from the North who wanted African Americans to be in school, have their own tools, and work on their own without being a sharecropper. He wanted all men to truly be equal. He and some other Republicans from the North decided to divide the Southern states into five **military districts**. They sent the military to each district to make sure the African Americans were being treated fairly. The military escorted them to school and made sure they were being treated fairly.

Figure 27

Military districts

Questions:

1. What was Lincoln's 10% plan? Explain.

2. What happened to Lincoln?

3. What was Presidential Reconstruction?

4. What was sharecropping?

5. What was the Freedmen's Bureau?

6.   What bad things happened during Presidential Reconstruction?

7.   Why were the Republicans in power in Congress during this time? Explain.

8.   What did the Republicans decide to do to make sure the African Americans were treated fairly?

9.   What is an easy way to remember the 13th amendment?

10.   What was Congressional Reconstruction?

PROJECT!

Create a picture of a road that includes all the events and plans for the Reconstruction period of the Civil War. Use pictures to show what was happening, and a key or bullet points to explain further. This can be labeled, "THE ROAD TO RECONSTRUCTION".

WRITE!

What does it take to make a big plan successful? How does a big plan fail? Is it important to enforce the rules? Why or why not? Explain.

Alternative Writing Assignment: Lincoln had big plans for America after the Civil War. What went wrong?

Lesson 2.9 (A): 3 Important Amendments

During Presidential Reconstruction and Congressional Reconstruction, some important **amendments** were made to the U.S. Constitution. What does the word amendment mean? It means *change*. Here are the important changes that were made:

13th amendment: no more slavery (abolish slavery)
14th amendment: if a person was born in America, he could not be denied privileges.
15th amendment: black males had the right to vote **NOTE: sometimes voting is called **suffrage**.

Remember: the military occupied most of the Southern states during this reconstruction. They did this to make sure they followed the rules. The North viewed the South as **conquered provinces**. This means they had been conquered in war and were territories that must now follow the rules. What was the President doing during this time? Remember, Andrew Johnson was the Vice President before Lincoln was assassinated. He was now the President, and he was not really in control of the country because of the Republican North and everything they were trying to do with Congressional Reconstruction. He tried to **VETO** all the laws the Republicans were passing in Congress (veto means to stop). Congress was able to pass every single law, so Johnson really had no power.

The **Northern Republican Congress** started to see what Andrew Johnson was trying to do - stop the Southern states from following the law. They were angry and tried to **impeach** him. This means they were trying to kick him out of the Presidency. Meanwhile, there were people from the Northern states who wanted to move to the Southern states and take advantage of the situation by getting some land of their own and trying to become wealthy. These people were nicknamed **carpetbaggers**.

The carpetbaggers were made fun of in the newspaper for traveling to the Southern states with their bags made from scraps of material, trying to get rich. There were some people from the Northern states that were trying to help, though. Like teachers that wanted to help by teaching African Americans how to read and write.

As the Northerners were coming South, there were also some Southerners who were taking advantage of the situation. Some rich Southerners made deals with some of the carpetbaggers to make money with the Northerners. They were made fun of for doing this (supporting the North), and they were called **Scalawags**.

Figure 28

THE MAN WITH THE (CARPET) BAGS
The bag in front of him, filled with others' faults, he always sees. The one behind him, filled with his own faults, he never sees.

Carpetbagger

Questions:
1. What was the 13th amendment?
2. What was the 14th amendment?
3. What was the 15th amendment?
4. What is an amendment?
5. Why couldn't Andrew Johnson veto the laws Congress was trying to pass?

6. Why did the American people want Johnson impeached?

7. What did a carpetbagger want?

8. What did a scalawag do?

WRITE!

Imagine you are a person living in the North and you heard about the new programs in the South during Reconstruction. Write a letter to a friend or family member to try to convince them to pack up everything and head South to set up a new life there. Of course, you are playing the part of carpetbagger here. Don't forget to include all the reasons why this would be a good idea.

PROJECT!

Use construction paper to re-create an image of a carpetbagger and of a scalawag. On the back, write what each of these types of people did during the Reconstruction era. Keep this in your journal.

Lesson 2.9 (B) : Progress Becomes Lost

As reconstruction continued with all the chaos of carpetbaggers, scalawags, military occupation of the Southern states, a President who had no real control, and an angry country, some progress was being made. For one thing, many African Americans became Congressmen in the Southern states. Most of the South was very upset about this. **Resistance groups** started to form, and this was very bad. The first group was called the **KKK, or Ku Klux Klan.** These white men dressed in white sheets and burned the homes of African Americans, beat, and killed African Americans, and tried to spread hatred against them.

At some point, most of the Northern population started to feel sorry for the South and everything they were going through. Some of the carpetbaggers who never had anything while living in the North were becoming wealthy and even being elected to political positions in the South. This made the Republican North feel like they were losing some of their power.

It was time for a Presidential election. The two men running for president were **Samuel Tilden** and **Rutherford B. Hayes**. Samuel Tilden represented the Democratic South, and he won the electoral votes over Rutherford B. Hayes who represented the Republican North. The Northerners felt for sure that they were now losing their power because they lost this presidential election, which took place in 1876.

So, what did they do? The Northerners sat down with the Southerners and tried to make a deal. They said they would take all the military districts that were in the Southern states away, plus they would take all the carpetbaggers away if they would just let their guy become President! And guess what? This is what happened! So, the man that lost, **Rutherford B. Hayes**, became President after all. This was officially called **The Compromise of 1877.**

With the carpetbaggers removed and all the military districts taken away in this deal, the South went right back to what it was doing before. All the help that was put into place for the slaves was taken away. **Jim Crow Laws** were soon passed in the South, which prevented African Americans from shopping and drinking where white Americans could, and even stopped them from voting!

Questions:

1.   What is a resistance group?

2.   What did the KKK do?

3.   What happened in the election between Samuel Tilden and Rutherford B. Hayes?

4.   What did the Northerners promise to do for the South if they would let their guy have the Presidency?

5.   What happened after the Compromise of 1877?

6.   What were the Jim Crow Laws?

PROJECT!

Create a slide presentation that shows the hopes of President Abraham Lincoln, how those hopes became lost after his assassination, the Reconstruction efforts, and how progress became lost by the end of 1877. Use lots of pictures and a few words in your presentation. Be confident to explain what happened in your own words when you present to the class.

Lesson 2.9 (C): A Low Point for America

What is **nadir**? It is a word that means the lowest point. This time just after Reconstruction was the lowest point for America. (The nadir of America) Jim Crow Laws were thriving in the South. This kept the African Americans separated from everything, every opportunity. There was **lynching** that happened. Lynching is a terrible thing. It meant that African Americans were beaten and hung from trees, just for being black. The year was early 1900's. This was the 20th century. There were some Presidents that tried to fix everything, but they were largely unsuccessful.

There were some notable people who advocated for change during this time. These people were known as **reformers**. They tried to create change.

Figure 29

Booker T. Washington: He grew up into slavery. He became an African American leader who created **The Tuskegee Institute**, which was a college and vocational training center for African Americans.
He believed that African Americans should be given a fair opportunity to make money. He believed that for the slaves they should be economically stable, basically to have money. He thought they should have tools to work the land if they wanted. He tried to get people in power to help him. He believed that the African Americans needed money more than they needed power. In a meeting called **The Atlanta Compromise** he tried to get them to agree to take away the power of voting for African Americans in exchange for economic opportunity.

Figure 30

W.E.B. DuBois wanted power before work for the African Americans. He created the **NAACP** (The National Association for the Advancement of Colored People) He was a very smart man. He graduated from Harvard University. He wanted the African Americans to have the power to vote so they would have rights. He believed this was more powerful for them than money.

Figure 31

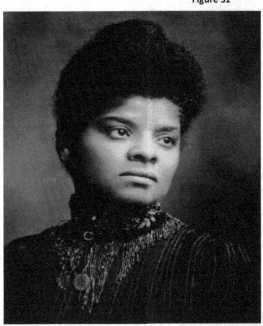

Ida B. Wells Barnett: She was a **muckraker**. This means a writer who wrote the truth - even the very bad, hard things that were happening in the world.

She wanted to expose to the world what was happening to the African Americans in our country. She wrote about the lynching. People all over the world read it in horror.

Marcus Garvey: He supported the idea that African Americans should just go back to Africa and leave America.

He supported **black nationalism**: Be proud to be black.

Figure 32

Questions:

1. What is nadir?
2. How was this time period the nadir of America? Give examples.

WRITE/PROJECT!

Research one of the reformers from this section. Create an informational graphic, movie, slide presentation, or paper explaining what they did to try to help. Include any interesting facts or background information you find through your research that would be relevant and/or enhance the presentation.

UNIT 3: CAPITALISM & REFORM
Lesson 3.1: The West During the Civil War and Reconstruction

At this point, you understand that there was a Civil War in America, followed by a period of Reconstruction. But where was this war and reconstruction taking place? It was happening in the North and the South. This next part of history explores what was happening at the same exact time but in the western part of America.

Westward expansion was still going on during the Civil War and Reconstruction period. This means that people were still moving West and gaining new land even though at the exact same time there was a war happening. Guess what? There were some major improvements going on in the West while this war was going on. One of those improvements was the creation of a **National Bank**. This made it possible for American people to borrow money from the government and pay the money back over time. This system enabled some Americans to get very, very wealthy during this time period.

Figure 33

Another major improvement was the creation of the railroad. People were taking resources from the West and using the railroad to send the goods to the East. Because there was no trading with other countries during this time, America was getting very wealthy by doing this. How? Because all the money was staying inside the country.

During the **secession** (when the South left America), the American government was able to control the entire country, with the majority of Congress Republican. Remember: The Southern States were mainly Democratic, but they had left the country during this time, so the Republicans were in power. The Republicans believed in **Hamiltonian Economics** (the National Bank, the creation of the railroad, and the trading within America), and this is what was happening in the West.

Remember all that new land that was acquired during Westward Expansion? Well, the government owned all that land, of course. But what they did was give that land to people for free. Back then, people could get 160 acres of land out West for free. This was called a **Land Grant**. But, of course, nothing is ever *really free*.

In exchange for the free land, the government wanted the people to develop the land and then send the resources from that land to the government. The government gave the people about 160 acres of land and a small house in exchange for the resources. This was called **The Homestead Act.**

How did the people get the resources? They worked the land by farming or raising cattle (cows), etc., and then sent the resources from that land to the government to use. Example: A cattle farm slaughters their cows, then sends the meat by railroad to Americans in other areas like the East. The railroad made everything much faster because the only other way to transport anything was by horse and wagon.

Figure 34

A typical house on the "free land"

But there is more. About 600,000 families in America were excited about this free land. They packed everything they had and moved West. Once they got settled and it was time to work the land, they needed things like tools and equipment, right? How did they get this? They borrowed money from the National Bank and bought the tools they needed, then they had to pay the money back in **payments with interest.** Interest is extra money charged by the bank for the loan. So, with this system, America was profiting big money because they were making money from the payment of the loans, and they were able to get supplies and resources from the new land, which was sold to people. All these factors made America very, very wealthy.

Questions:

1. What was happening during the Civil War and Reconstruction period out West?

2. What was the National Bank?

3. Why were Republicans able to take over Congress during this time period? Explain.

4. What were some main points of Hamiltonian Economics?

5. Explain the land grants.

6. What did the people have to do when they needed to buy equipment and tools to work the land?

7. How did the National Bank profit from the people?

60

8.   How many Americans wanted to go out West for free land?

9.   Why was the railroad so important?

10.   Do you agree with Hamiltonian Economics or not? Why?

PROJECT!

Draw a map of the United States on a piece of paper. Now, create graphics on the map that represent all the parts of Hamiltonian Economics. (railroad, National Bank, trading only within America, etc.) Also include Homestead Act and Land Grants along with the Factory North on the map. Use a key to give more information about what is on the map. Don't forget to include the fact that the South was The Confederate States of America during this time.

Lesson 3.2: Building the Transcontinental Railroad

The United States government was very interested in building the railroad. Why? Because remember, the railroad would help connect the West with the East for fast transport of goods. To speed up the process of getting the railroad tracks built, the government offered the American people free land and money to lay railroad tracks. Here was the deal they offered:

Railroad Companies were given some land. They were given some money (**subsidies**) and supplies to build the railroad tracks on the land.
For each square mile of track built, the government would pay the landowner money. After the tracks were finished the landowner could do whatever they wanted with the land.

This "deal" was called **The Pacific Railway Act of 1862.** But the Railroad Company owners took advantage of this deal. How? Some people lied to the government about how much track they were laying in order to get more money. Some people made the track longer on purpose just to get more money. So instead of laying the track in a straight line, they went in a curvy pattern to get more money.

Figure 35

Working on the track.

When the railroad was finished it linked the Eastern part of the United States with the Western part. What used to take three months to transport by covered wagon now took only about six days! This railroad allowed the United States to have its own market called a **National Market**. The railroad was called **The Transcontinental Railroad.** This national market allowed the United States to trade within the country, and not trade with any other countries. How did it work, actually?

Natural resources from the West (like the meat from cattle farms) were being shipped to the factories in the East (for the meat to be processed). Once the factories had the goods processed, they used the railroad to ship the goods all over the country for people to buy.

Questions:

1.   How did the government work out a deal to lay railroad track very quickly?

2.   Why was the government motivated to lay railroad tracks from the West to the East? Explain.

3.   What was the benefit for an American to lay a railroad track? Explain.

4.   How did the people take advantage of the deal the government was offering?

5.   Explain or draw a picture of the National Market.

6.   Explain the process of moving natural resources from the West to the East.

7.   What was the railroad called?

8.   What was happening in America at the same time that the railroad was being built?

9.   If you could go back in time to this era in America, where would you choose to live? Why?

WRITE!

In your journal, expand on the question in number 9. Let thoughts run freely through your mind and onto your notebook paper or tablet.

Lesson 3.3: The Farmers, The Buffalo, & The Native Americans

Figure 36

During this time of building the railroad, there were groups of people making lots of money and getting very rich. The railroad was becoming very rich. Think about it: every time they operated the railroad to move goods, they charged money.

The steel companies were also getting rich. They were the ones supplying all the steel to build the railroad tracks. The steel factories were in the North. They made lots of money.

The big businesses were also getting rich because now they could offer products to more people at a faster pace. But who wasn't making money? The farmer. The common farmer was working hard, but always owing money to keep everything going. They were working so hard to keep up, but they were not making much money at all.

The Credit Mobilier Scandal: This was when a very big railroad company called the **Union Pacific Railroad** formed another company called ***The Credit Mobilier of America***. This company gave all the contracts to build the railroad to the Union Pacific Railroad so they could get all the business. They also sold or gave away stock in their company to government officials so they could get rich, too. These government officials were motivated to give the Union Pacific Railroad all the government money to build more track and expand the railroad because they would benefit financially from this. What else was happening? Well, the **buffalo (or bison)** were being killed in very large numbers during this time. Let's look in to this a little deeper. The buffalo were these large, large animals that could be found all over the West in America.

The Native Americans used the meat for food and their skin for building shelter and clothing. But this is not why they were disappearing in very large numbers. The building of the railroad killed the buffalo. How? Because when they were building the tracks, they built the tracks right where the buffalo lived. Once the trains started moving, they would hit the buffalo all the time. This would stop the trains from moving because these animals were so large. They would have to stop and clean everything up to keep the train moving. To solve this problem the government hired men to hunt and kill the buffalo. Within about 30 years they were almost extinct. (gone)

Because of what was happening to the buffalo, the **Native Americans (or Indians)** were dying. The **Plains Indians** were destroyed because of this because they depended on the buffalo to live. What was left of them (the Indians), were gathered up by the United States government and they were put on new land called **reservations**.

But guess what happened next? They found gold on that new land. Because the American government wanted that gold, they relocated the Indians again so they could get the gold. The **Sioux Indians** were tired of getting pushed around during this time, so they started **The Indian Wars**. Guess what the United States government did about this? They got **General Sherman** (remember him?) to go out West and kill the Indians. Some of the famous battles of the Indian Wars were **The Battle of Little Bighorn** and **Custer's Last Stand.** The American government also gave some of the land that belonged to the Native Americans to other people.

They created **The Dawes Act of 1887** that gave away their land to individual families and relocated them to the reservations. They even sent them to schools where they had to wear uniforms and try to learn like the white man. One school was in Pennsylvania called **The Carlisle Indian School**. This happened between 1879-1918. The last major conflict between the Native Americans and the United States military was in 1890 and it was called the **Wounded Knee Massacre**.

Questions:

1. Explain how the railroad, the steel companies, and the businesses were getting rich during this time.

2. What was the credit mobilier company?

3. How did the credit mobilier company get rich? Explain.

4. Why were the buffalo a problem for the railroad companies?

5. What did the government do to control the buffalo?

6. Why did the Indians start to die?

7. What was the name of where the American government moved the Indians?

8. What did they do with their land?

9. What happened when gold was found on the new land?

10. What was the Carlisle School?

11. Why did the Indian Wars happen?

WRITE!

Imagine you are a Native American during this time. Write a letter to a family member explaining what has happened to you, including what you think of your new school.

Lesson 3.4: Government Loves Big Business

The economic growth of the United States gave the country a status of being an **Industrial Power**. This means that the U.S. had:

- A huge number of natural resources.
- Government support and protection. (they helped the inventors and businesses become successful)
- Railroad subsidies (the government helped pay for the railroad)
- Tariffs (prevented trade from other countries)
- Labor policies (allowing immigrants to come to America to work)

With more money comes more power. This time period in America was called **The Gilded Age**. The government was helping **entrepreneurs** (people who had a new idea for a business) and inventors to make new things. They would loan them money to get their business started. When they paid back the loan, they paid **interest** (money paid to the bank for letting them borrow the money).

The National Bank was becoming rich off this. Gold, coal, and iron were found in the West. Anything that got in the way of getting more gold, coal, and iron was killed or destroyed by the government.

Patent laws were passed to protect the ideas of inventors from getting stolen or copied by others. The invention of the **steam engine** was huge. It enabled people and companies to run things much faster and more efficiently, which made them even more money.

At this time, the Republican party was in control of America because the South, where all the Democrats were in power had seceded from America during the Civil War. With the Republicans in total charge of America, they promoted economic growth.

In a famous court case called **Gibbons v. Ogden** the Supreme Court ruled that states could not interfere with national business. The government always protected big business.

Open Immigration happened to allow immigrants to come to America from other countries to work in the factories and the railroad. Many people came from China to build the railroad.

After the railroad was built, America passed **The Chinese Exclusion Act** which meant they must go back to China, even though they had made a home for themselves in America. Bottom line: the government supported big business and not the worker!

All this growth and money led to a big **surplus** of products being produced (too much of one product). Because America had a protective tariff that did not allow them to trade with other countries, there was nowhere to sell the huge number of products that were being made. This is when America started to look at opening trade with other countries again - to get rid of the massive number of products that were being produced. So, they lowered the taxes to be able to start trading with other countries again. They opened the borders and created an **international trade**.

Questions:

1. What were some natural resources that were found in the West?

2. How did the government help the inventors and entrepreneurs?

3. How did the government stop America from trading with other countries?

4. Explain open immigration and why America did this.

5. What was the time period called when America was becoming an industrial power?

6. How did the National Bank work? Explain.

7. What did the invention of the steam engine do for big business? Explain.

8. How did America end up with a surplus of products?

9. How did America solve the problem of too much product?

10. Explain the Chinese Exclusion Act. Explain the case, Gibbons v. Ogden.

WRITE/PROJECT!

Research some of the most notable entrepreneurs of this time period. Create an informational graphic about your favorite entrepreneur including everything you've learned about his/her life and invention or idea. This project can be a slide presentation, a large poster, or a movie!

Lesson 3.5: The Factors of Production & Capitalism

You know by now that the government supported "big businesses". They did not support the worker. **The Factors of Production** are all the things that go together to produce a product. (the seed company, the farmer, the tool company, the harvesting of crops, the packaging, and the transport to finally sell in a store).

Capitalism is being allowed to have economic freedom so that products can be made, new inventions can happen, and the opportunity to make money is there. The American government supported capitalism.

During the Gilded Age, (that is the time period we are talking about in this standard) new towns and cities started to rise up right in the areas where the railroads were being built. There were small businesses that popped up along the railroad routes and those businesses thrived (did great).

There were restaurants, laundries, shopping areas, and all kinds of small businesses that supported the towns and cities. The railroad was very powerful because wherever they were, there was money and there was growth.

Some small business owners made good money, but some made huge money and became multi- billionaires.

Figure 37

One man was named **Andrew Carnegie**. He was an inventor and a businessman. He used something called **The Bessemer Process** to make steel very quickly and efficiently. What are railroad tracks made of? You guessed it - steel! His biggest customer was the railroad, and he got very rich.

What Andrew Carnegie did was that he bought his own railroad company. That's how much money he had! So, he made the steel for the railroad, he owned his own railroad company, he transported the steel to other companies that needed it, and he made money on every single part of the steel industry. When this happens, it is called **Vertical Integration.** (When a company takes over every aspect of an industry)

Figure 38

Figure 39

Andrew Carnegie (L) & John D. Rockefeller (R)

Another man who became very rich during the Gilded Age was **John D. Rockefeller**. He made big money in the oil industry.

What he did was he tried to control every aspect of the oil business. He controlled all the stores that sold gas and made them only sell his products.

He made his stores sell gas at the cheapest price, so no one would shop at any other gas stores. Those other stores went out of business. As soon as they went out of business, he increased his prices.

This process is called **Horizontal Integration**. (the merging of companies that sell similar products, when someone buys every company that sells the same thing and then controls the prices).

A **business monopoly** is when one company has complete control over an entire industry, so there is no competition. During this time, John D. Rockefeller was trying to **monopolize** the oil industry.

Mr. Rockefeller and others like him were referred to as **robber barons** by the American people because they saw that these men were able to basically rob the people and get rich off what they were doing, and the government would always protect them.

One way they were protected was by helping them form a **trust**, which is a fake company that protects the real company from a lawsuit. The **Sherman Anti-Trust Act** was passed that made it illegal to form a trust that interfered with free trade between states or with other countries. Because the government loved and supported big business, this law had very little impact on the situation.

Questions:

1. What is capitalism?

2. How did small businesses survive during the Gilded Age? Explain.

3. What did Andrew Carnegie invent? Explain.

4. How did Andrew Carnegie practice "vertical integration"? Explain.

5. What is "horizontal integration"? Explain.

6. What did John D. Rockefeller do to make so much money?

7. What is a monopoly?

8. What did the American people call the rich business owners? Why?

9. What is a trust?

10. How did the government try to write a law to stop the rich business owners from violating a trust? Did it work?

WRITE/PROJECT!

Think of one of your favorite products. Now, do some research on all the steps it takes to create this product. Is every part of the product made in the same place? If not, track the places/factories where each part of the product originates and how it all comes together to sell on the market. Create an infographic, slide show, or poster to show what you've learned!

Lesson 3.6: Philanthropy

Philanthropy is the giving away of money. The rich, rich guys like **Andrew Carnegie, John D. Rockefeller,** and **J.P. Morgan** (he made big money in banking), were all trying to monopolize their industry. Some Americans called them the **robber barons**, but others called them **The Captains of Industry**. People believed that there were some that were so smart and so good at business matters, that they were "meant to be" rich, and the "captains" of their industries. Psychologists called this **Social Darwinism**. This means that the psychologists believed that they were the best in their industries, and it was "meant to be" that they became the richest.

The workers that kept these companies going didn't make much money, while the captains of industry got very rich. The business owners started to feel a little guilty and wanted to be remembered as doing good things for America, rather than just get remembered for being super wealthy, so they started to give their money away. (This is called **philanthropy**).

Andrew Carnegie started this idea, and he called it **The Gospel of Wealth**. He said he wanted to do good things for the American people with all his money so he would be remembered by people in a good way.

Andrew Carnegie started building libraries all over America. Others built buildings with their money that the American people could use for fun. There were buildings like libraries, music halls, and educational buildings. These men gave away a lot of their money so they could be remembered for doing something good for people. It worked, too!

Figure 40   Figure 41

New technologies of the Gilded Age.

The American people almost idolized them. They looked up to them, tried to dress like them and everything. Because electricity had just been invented, the telephone, the typewriter, and other inventions were happening, the American people were enjoying a new standard of living. With so many telephones and other inventions being mass produced in the factories, the prices of these goods went down. More people could afford these luxuries, and this made them feel good, like a Rockefeller!

Questions:

1. What is philanthropy?

2. What did psychologists say about the super wealthy?

3. What was the Gospel of Wealth?

4. What types of things did the rich business owners do for the American people?

5. How was the standard of living getting better for the American people during this time?

WRITE!

If you had unlimited money, what would you do to be philanthropic? Write your ideas down in your journal and discuss with a partner.

Lesson 3.7: The Farmers and The Laborers

The government always took the side of big business and they controlled everything. The farmers and the laborers, though, were barely making it. They made just enough to pay their bills, but that was all. One of the problems was **supply and demand**. The faster goods were produced, the more products were in supply.

There were more products in America than there was demand or people who wanted to buy those products. This created a surplus of products, which meant the prices on the products went down. The farmers experienced a surplus of crops during this time. The supply of the crops was so great that the prices went down. This meant that the farmers made less money on the sale of their crops. What did they do about this? They planted more crops to try to make up for the cheaper prices - but this did not help at all. It made things worse for them.

The farmers and the laborers got together and organized a group called **The Grange**. They were basically against the railroad companies because the railroad transported their crops, but they charged them a lot of money to do this. They blamed the railroad for all their economic problems. Some state legislatures passed laws called **The Granger Laws** which tried to regulate how much the railroad companies could charge for the transportation of their crops.

The Granger Laws did not work because of a Supreme Court case called **Gibbons v. Ogden** that would not allow a State to interfere with business (commerce) that was considered National business (crossed state lines). This case made it impossible for the individual states to regulate anything to do with the railroad because the railroad was involved in national business.

Further, the Supreme Court ruled that states could not interfere with railroad rates at all because they crossed state lines all the time. This case was called **Munn v. Illinois.** The United States did pass the **Interstate Commerce Act** to control the rates and practices of the railroad, but the farmers and laborers still were not getting enough help.

Next, they created their own political party called **The People's Party**, sometimes called **The Populist Party**. They did this to attempt to influence the national government, the railroads, banking, and currency (money). The Populist Party wanted to make the economy based on silver instead of everything based on gold because there wasn't much gold, but there was a lot of silver. They thought if they did this more people would have money.

They believed that by increasing the amount of silver mined and turned into coins that would help them to get higher prices for their goods. This idea was called **bimetallism.** If they made their money based on two metals, there would be more. Well, that did not work. Money is still based on gold.

The Populist Party did get some things accomplished, though. They were able to pass that Senators would be elected by popular vote. This was the **17th Amendment**. They were also able to pass laws that said voting in elections should be done by **secret ballot**, this way no one could see who a person was voting for.

One more important thing they accomplished was creating a **graduated income tax**. This meant that the more money a person earned, the more taxes they had to pay. The less money a person earned, the less taxes they had to pay. They also partnered with the laborers to try to advocate for an 8-hour workday.

Questions:
1. Explain the problem of supply and demand for the farmers and laborers.

2. What is a surplus of goods?
3. What happens to the price of goods when there is a surplus?
4. What did the farmers and laborers do to try to fight the railroad?

5. Why was the railroad protected?

6. What new Supreme Court case stopped the states from regulating the railroad?

7. Explain the idea of bimetallism.

8. What was the 17th amendment?

9. What was a secret ballot?

10. Explain graduated income tax.

WRITE!

Think of ways the farmers and laborers helped their cause. In the end, how did these ideas help future farmers and workers? Explain.

Lesson 3.8: The Factory Workers

We know that the farmers and laborers were suffering during this time, but there was another group of workers who were suffering: the factory workers. The big money guys (remember the robber barons, the Captains of Industry) were making the factory workers' jobs very difficult. They were working very long hours in the factories to produce goods faster and faster.

They were not making enough money to have fun. They were working all the time and barely able to just pay the bills, while the robber barons were getting rich, along with the support of the government.

The factory workers created **Labor Unions**. This was a group of workers who elected union leaders who would go in and negotiate with the big factories to get better working conditions and higher wages for the workers.

If the labor unions did not get what they wanted, sometimes they would urge the workers to stop working. This was called a **strike**. The idea was that if they did not work, goods would not be produced, and the big factories would have to give them what they wanted to keep things going.

The government protected the factories, though, and just hired more workers to go do the job. These new workers were called **scabs** because they were looked down upon for supporting the government during a strike.

If a worker wanted to work during a strike, he had to sign a contract called a **yellow dog contract**. This said that they would not go on strike, no matter what happened. If the worker still went on strike anyway, he would get **black- listed**. This meant that his name went on a list, and he would never get hired again!

The government did not like the big labor unions. They always supported big business. One strike that happened during this time was **The Railroad Strike of 1877**. The railroad workers stopped working, but the government sided with the railroad companies, not the workers.

There was a protest that was against police in Chicago for being too rough with the citizens. This was called **The Haymarket Incident**. Then there was the **Pullman Strike**, which was another railroad strike where the workers were demanding higher pay. The government sided with the railroad and the protestors were thrown in jail!

The government labeled union members as dangerous, radical communists. One successful union was called **The Craft Union**. This was a group of workers who had a special, specific skill that not just anyone could do. Because the skilled worker was difficult to replace with just anybody, they had some power and usually got what they wanted. However, not a lot of people joined the unions back then because they didn't totally understand them and were afraid of what would happen.

There was a Presidential election during this time (1896) with a Populist candidate running in support of the workers and laborers. His name was **William Jennings Bryan**. He said that the gold was like a "crown of thorns" that was made to hurt the common, working man. He ran against **William McKinley**, who supported big business and was a republican. He called upon the big businessmen to help him win the election and it worked, but the door was open for change.

Questions:

1. Why were the factory workers unhappy?

2. Who did they blame for their problems?
3. What did they do to try to get better working conditions?

4. What is a strike? Name two important strikes.

5. What is a scab?

6. What was a yellow dog contract?

7. What did it mean to be black-listed?

8. Why was the Craft Union successful? Explain.

9. What was the "crown of thorns"?

10. How did William McKinley win the Presidential election?

WRITE!

Imagine you are at work and most of your co-workers went on strike. What would you do in this situation? Explain your reasons and then share with a partner.

Lesson 3.9: The Immigrants

Figure 43

An ethnic neighborhood in New York City.

Many of the immigrants who were coming to America during this time were excited about their new life in a new country. However, it was difficult for them to leave everything they knew. For example, they missed their language, their food, their churches, their schools, and their way of life.

Once the immigrants were settled in their new city, they began to band together and form communities. In these communities they formed their own markets, schools, churches, and neighborhoods. These neighborhoods were called **ethnic neighborhoods** because they were separated by ethnicity.

Today, these ethnic neighborhoods still thrive, and tourists that visit the big cities often enjoy visiting to experience different cultures. They enjoy shopping and eating authentic Italian, Greek, Chinese, or German food, depending on the ethnic neighborhood they visit. These neighborhoods helped the immigrants to feel that they were bringing a piece of their own culture to their new country.

Why did the immigrants come to America during this time? Many felt pushed out of their countries and pulled towards America during the Gilded Age because of all the jobs, progress, and opportunity. The United States opened the border to the West to allow Asian immigrants to come in to work on building the railroad.

The farmers who were out West started moving into the bigger cities in search of jobs. The immigrants also went to the cities because that is where all the jobs were. New immigrants were also coming from southeastern and eastern Europe from countries like Poland, Russia, Italy, Greece, and Ireland. They represented a mixture of different religions such as Catholic, Orthodox, and Jewish.

The cities were already crowded because that is where the jobs were, and there was new technology and always things to do. Back then, the cities had big skyscrapers (very tall buildings) and even railroads built up high. The cities were crowded with people looking for jobs and wanting to be around all that technology and excitement. Now with the immigrants coming in the cities are even more crowded. The rise of immigrants coming to America was between 1890-1920.

The Americans did not like the immigrants coming in because they were taking their jobs. They were willing to work for less money. They did not speak English, and the Americans did not like this. They also practiced different kinds of religions than they were used to, and this made them uncomfortable.

Figure 44

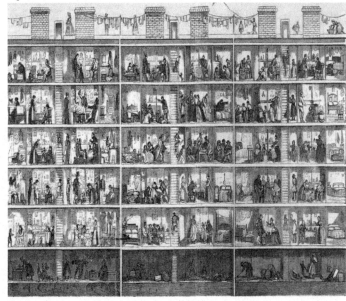

A drawing of the inside of a tenement building.

The immigrants started to create their own **ethnic neighborhoods** in the cities. They often had to share crowded housing to be able to afford to live in their new country.

This housing was called a **tenement**, and the living conditions were not good at all. This is a picture of the inside of a typical tenement.

These neighborhoods are still thriving today in cities like Chicago, New York, and San Francisco. The immigrants also voted in elections. They voted for the candidate who helped find them jobs and helped to support their way of life in America. But the American people only really supported the immigrants coming from Ireland and England, mainly because they spoke English.

There were political leaders in the cities that were able to solve important problems in the ethnic neighborhoods. The immigrants were not always treated fairly at their jobs. There was a famous ward boss in New York named **William "Boss" Tweed** who did not treat them fairly.

Many political leaders would exchange homes and jobs to immigrants for their vote. This happened a lot, but the houses were very crowded with 8-10 people in a room and only 1 bathroom. These overcrowded houses were called **tenements**.

Their workplaces were often called **sweatshops** because of the hot, sweaty, dirty working conditions with long hours and little to no breaks.

There were some muckrakers (people who wrote the truth) who wrote about the poor living and working conditions of the immigrants. One was named **Jacob Riis**. He took pictures of the tenements and sweatshops to show the public what was happening.

Upton Sinclair was another who dressed up like a worker and got a job in the meatpacking factories. He took pictures and wrote about the dirty and unsanitary meatpacking industry in a book called **The Jungle** and published those for all to see.

NOTES:

Another group that was moving to the cities during this time was the African Americans. The newly freed slaves were moving to the cities away from the Southern plantations in search of work in the factories. This was called **The Great Migration**. This is when the African Americans started to not only move North, but also to the West and Midwest. The African Americans and the immigrants were treated the worst. They were the last to be hired and the first to be fired from jobs. They were the workers they brought in during the strikes and they lived in the worst part of the cities. Life was very hard for them.

After the railroad was built, the government created the **Chinese Exclusion Act of 1882** which forced the Chinese immigrants to leave America. The United States was becoming a huge melting pot of different cultures, traditions, languages, and food. Basically, America was very exciting during the Gilded Age and many people from all over the world wanted to come.

Figure 45

Women working in a sweatshop.

NOTES:

Questions:

1. Why did the immigrants want to come to America? What years did they move to America in great numbers?

2. What was the Chinese Exclusion Act?

3. What was a sweatshop?

4. What was a tenement?

5. What is an ethnic neighborhood? Give some examples.

6. Why were the cities so attractive and exciting at this time?

7. Who were the muckrakers who wrote about the conditions for the immigrants?

8. Why didn't the Americans want the immigrants there?

9. Who were the groups that Americans tolerated the most? Why?

10. How did the immigrants have some power, politically?

PROJECT!

Mini-Research Opportunity: Research some ethnic neighborhoods in America. Where would you like to visit? What can you do there? Create an itinerary for a trip there and present it in a movie, slideshow presentation, or poster.

Lesson 3.9 (A): Reform

As in the past, there were reformers who fought for change. One reformer was **Jane Addams**. She helped the immigrants find houses - good houses. She had one place called **Hull House**. Immigrants could go there and receive childcare, job training and a welcome. It was like a community center for immigrants.

Figure 46

Upton Sinclair

Another reformer was **Upton Sinclair**. He was a writer who wrote a book called *The Jungle*.

It exposed the unclean working environment of the meatpacking industry.

This prompted **The Progressive Movement** which aimed to clean up the meatpacking industry and the tenement housing.

Two presidents, **Teddy Roosevelt** and **Woodrow Wilson** tried to make things better for the laborers and the farmers.

Roosevelt offered Americans a **Fair Deal,** promising to punish the big businesses that didn't treat people fairly. Roosevelt also was responsible for creating the **Pure Food and Drug Act** and **The Meat Inspection Act** to make sure the food and drugs were safe for people to eat. He also started his own political party called **The Bull Moose Party** and it split the Republican Party.

Roosevelt became known as a **Trust Buster**. He would stand up to big businesses and side with the worker. He was the first President to stand up for the workers in a strike called the **Anthracite Coal Strike.** He was also known as the creator of America's **National Park** system. These are huge tracts of land all over America where people can enjoy nature.

Woodrow Wilson created the **Clayton Antitrust Act** that strengthened the **Sherman Antitrust Act**. This regulated the trusts that were there to protect big businesses from being sued and attempted to end monopolies. He also created the **Child Labor Legislation** that made it unconstitutional for children to go to work.

Finally, he created the **Federal Reserve Act** which was a central banking system that regulated how much interest rates to charge the people.

The important amendments to the constitution during the Gilded Age were:

16th Amendment: This is when the Populist party created a graduated federal income tax. (easy way to remember this: when you are 16 is when you usually start working - AND paying federal income taxes out of your check!)

17th Amendment: The election of Senators by popular vote. (Easy way to remember this: 17 is a boring age, senators can also be boring.....)

18th Amendment: Prohibition of alcohol (no more drinking!) Easy way to remember this: you cannot legally drink alcohol if you are 18 years old.

19th Amendment: Women got the right to vote. (easy way to remember this.....finally, after 19 million years women get some rights!)

Important to Note: **Alice Paul** and **Carrie Chapman Catt** were known as the **Suffragettes**. They helped get the 19th amendment passed for women to vote. Suffrage=voting.

Questions:

1. What did Jane Addams do for reform?

2. What book did Upton Sinclair write and what was it about?

3. What was the Progressive Movement?

4. How did Teddy Roosevelt stand up to big businesses for the workers? Give examples.

5. What else did Teddy Roosevelt do for America?

6. What were the Anti-Trust Acts that Woodrow Wilson helped pass?

7. What else did Woodrow Wilson do for America?

8. What is an easy way to remember the 19th amendment?

9. What is an easy way to remember the 17th amendment?

10. What is an easy way to remember the 18th amendment?

11. What is an easy way to remember the 16th amendment?

PROJECT!

Mini-Research Opportunity: Research some of America's National Parks. What interests you the most? What types of things can you do there? Create an itinerary for a trip there and present it in a slideshow, movie, or poster.

Unit 4: MODERNISM AND INTERVENTION
Lesson 4.1: American Imperialism 1867-1914

Now that you know all about what was happening in the new land out West, we are going to look at how America was interacting with the rest of the world during this same time period. We'll start with the surplus problem in America with too many crops and not enough people to sell them to. The only thing to do here was to open the borders to trade with foreign countries. The idea of keeping everything in one country is called **isolationism**. When a country engages with other countries, this is called **imperialism**.

In 1867 America was convinced by a congressman named Seaward to buy Alaska. Once it was purchased there was no more land left to buy in North America. America seemed to have it all- money and power and land….and getting a little bored. This is when America started to venture out into other countries to see what resources they had that they could benefit from.

Figure 47

There was an idea known as **Social Darwinism** which said that because America was "better" than the other countries it was okay for them to just take things from other countries. Another idea that was similar to this one was called **Survival of the Fittest**. This means that the best man wins - the strongest man survives. This was the mindset of America during this time.

When America opened the borders to trade with other countries again the farmers finally had a place to send those extra crops. Now, the crop prices went back up and the farmers were happy again. Americans became settled and happy during this time, feeling like nothing could go wrong and they had great pride in being American.

In some other countries during this time, they were having some problems that many thought America should help them with. There was a big push to convert the world into **Christianity**. Some saw this as "The White Man's Burden". This is the belief that the white man had a responsibility to make everyone in the world like him. **Rudyard Kipling** was a famous writer who wrote a poem called **The White Man's Burden**. It was all about making the white people the citizens to model the world after.

To spread its power with the world, America started to create a lot of naval bases. The Navy was a sign of a country's power. How many naval bases a country had showed how powerful it was, so America started creating more and more naval bases. There was a Navy Admiral (someone high in rank with the Navy) named **Alfred Mahan**. He wrote a book called **The Influence of Sea Power Upon History**. Some of America's Presidents read this book and agreed with him. **Theodore Roosevelt** was one President that really believed in this power.

America went to Hawaii and set up a naval base there. The military just showed up, and there was a Queen there named **Liliuokalani.** America threw her out of leadership and overpowered the area and set up a naval base named **Pearl Harbor.** Other countries were seeing what America was doing and they were getting stressed. It created a lot of tension. Others were looking at America and building up hostility and resentment for what they were doing.

Figure 48

Questions:

1. What is isolationism?

2. What is imperialism?

3. When did we buy Alaska? How was this a turning point for America?

4. What was Social Darwinism?

5. What is Survival of the Fittest?

6. How did the farmers finally start making some money?

7. What was the White Man's Burden?

8. Why were naval bases so important to America?

9. What did America do to Hawaii?

10. How did other countries feel about what America was doing?

WRITE!

Think about how America went from the original 13 colonies to becoming an imperialistic nation wanting to conquer the world. Write your thoughts about this process in your journal. Don't forget to include any feelings about progress whether it be positive or negative.

Lesson 4.2: The Spanish American War

One of the situations that America got into was when they got involved with trying to help some countries get free from Spain. It was the end of the 1800's (end of the 19th century). Cuba was controlled by Spain during this time and America came to help them break away. They wrote a law called **The Teller Amendment** in 1898. This law allowed them to get Cuba to be independent from Spain.

How did they do it? America sent a big ship called **The USS Maine** down near Cuba to basically intimidate Spain. It basically showed them that "America was here." But something happened. The ship suddenly caught fire and blew up on February 15, 1898. The newspapers showed pictures of this and blamed it on Spain.

Figure 49   **What people saw in the newspaper.**

Joseph Pulitzer and **William Randolph Hearst** owned very big newspapers and they reported that Spain had blown up the USS Maine in **Havana Harbor**. But guess what? This was a lie. Actually, it was just a boiler problem inside the ship and that is why it caught on fire, but the lie that Spain attacked the ship sold lots more newspapers. This is called **yellow journalism**. One of the headlines was, "Remember the Maine, to Hell with Spain!"

Theodore Roosevelt (Teddy Roosevelt) was not the President during this time. He organized a group of volunteer soldiers called **The Rough Riders**. With his group, he fought Spain in a battle called **The Battle of San Juan Hill**. America continued to fight Spain in the Pacific Ocean (the Philippines) and in the Caribbean Ocean (in Cuba), and America won.

With this win, America inherited what was left of the Spanish Colonial Empire. They took **The Philippines, Guam, Puerto Rico,** and freed Cuba from Spanish rule. (The Teller Amendment said that America could only help Cuba, not own them). This war only lasted a couple of months. It is known as **The Spanish-American War.**

The Platt Amendment was written in 1901 and *it stated that America could control Cuba, but not own it.* This meant Cuba had to rely on what the United States told them to do. They put a naval base there known as **Guantanamo Bay**. Well, the new countries, The Philippines, Guam, Puerto Rico, and Cuba, wanted the same freedoms as America. They wanted to follow the United States Constitution. America said, no. Just because you fly our flag does not mean you have the same American freedoms. This was known as **The Insular Cases 1901-1905.**

This unfair treatment sparked many people to resent America for what they were doing. Some famous Americans like **Mark Twain, Andrew Carnegie, and William G. Sumner** formed the **Anti-Imperialist League**. They didn't like that America was taking territory and then not giving anything back. They felt that America was the land of the free. Mark Twain said that they were acting like pirates, just taking what they wanted. He said the American flag should be changed to a Pirate flag. The Imperialists disagreed. They said we should help all the other countries that needed us. The Anti-Imperialists said we were sacrificing our values to become a world power.

Questions:

1. What was the Teller Amendment?

2. What is yellow journalism?

3. How did yellow journalism start a war?

4. What group did Teddy Roosevelt form? What did they do?

5. What countries did America acquire after the Spanish-American War?

6. What stopped America from owning Cuba?

7.   What did the Platt Amendment state?

8.   What were the Insular Cases?

9.   What was the belief of the Anti-Imperialist League?

10. What did the Imperialists believe?

PROJECT!

Research information about relations between Cuba and America. Take notes. Next, look at your notes and create a presentation or infographic, poster or movie that will show the changes between these two countries through the years.

Lesson 4.3: Presidential Foreign Policy

With all the naval bases in so many different countries, America was in full imperialism mode. Remember, imperialism is when a country gets involved with another country. America was not the only country doing this at the time. England, Spain, and Germany were involved as well. These countries were going into China and taking things from them. America wanted to do this as well, so they created something called the **Open-Door Policy of 1899.** This said that America could go into China anytime they wanted even though other European countries were there first.

The Chinese reacted by using their martial arts skills against the Americans. This was called **The Boxer Rebellion (1899-1901).** It was unsuccessful because Americans used guns and shot at them.

Figure 50

There were 3 important Presidents during this time of imperialism in America, and they all had their own ideas of how to deal with the countries America was taking over and the people living in those countries. This is called **foreign policy**. It shows what each Presidential administration believes regarding foreign countries and our involvement with the people there. Here are some important examples:

Teddy Roosevelt: 1901-1909. His foreign policy was known as the "**Big Stick Policy**". He was famous for saying, *speak softly, carry a big stick, and use force if necessary.* He believed that controlling other countries by force was the way to go. He also wanted Europe to stay out of Latin America. This was called the **Roosevelt Corollary**. He believed in the power of the threat of *the great white fleet*, which was the naval ships everywhere. One final accomplishment for him was with **Panama**. This country was experiencing a revolt with Columbia at the time. He offered to help them win, which was successful. Then, he asked for a return favor. He wanted to use the land in Panama to cut a long canal to save ships time. This canal, called **The Panama Canal** allowed ships to bypass South America and go straight to the West coast of America in California.

Figure 51   The Panama Canal.

William H. Taft: 1909-1913. His foreign policy was known as the **Dollar Policy**. He believed if America would put money into Latin American countries that this would be a way to get the resources it wanted. He thought America should just purchase what it wanted with money and that this would protect American business interests in Latin America.

Woodrow Wilson: 1913-1921. His foreign policy was known as the **Moral Policy.** He believed in spreading Christianity to Latin America. If America went on missions to spread morals to Latin America, then this would promote democratic governments there.

Questions:

1. What is imperialism?

2. What is meant by foreign policy?

3. What other countries were involved in imperialism?

4. What was the Open-Door Policy?

5. How did China react to the Open-Door Policy? Explain.

6. What was the Big Stick Policy?

7. What did Woodrow Wilson believe we should do about Latin America?

8. What did William H. Taft believe we should do about Latin America?

PROJECT!

Create a poster for each of the three Presidents discussed in this section. The poster should reflect the President's foreign policy and include details to explain his beliefs. Imagine this poster as an advertisement to the people of America to inform them about each man's stance on foreign policy.

Lesson 4.4: World War I & The Propaganda of War

A war begins to break out in Europe because the heir to the throne of Austria-Hungary was assassinated. His name was **Archduke Franz Ferdinand**. He was assassinated in Sarajevo in Eastern Europe. When this happened, a war started. In Europe, there were **alliances**. This means that certain countries "stuck together" to help each other out.   So, when the assassination happened, the alliances banded together and started to fight against the other alliances.

Alliance examples: **Britain, France, and Russia**. Alliance called the **Triple Entente. Germany, Austria-Hungary, Italy**. Alliance called the **Triple Alliance**.

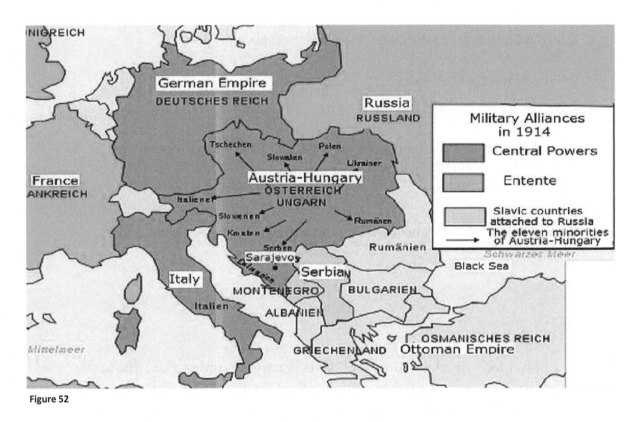

Figure 52

At first the United States did nothing. They did not want to get involved. But they did send guns and ammo over to England, Great Britain, and the United Kingdom. **GOOD TO KNOW**: *Great Britain* is England, Wales, and Scotland together. *The United Kingdom* is the union of all Great Britain plus Northern Ireland.

Then, a British cruise liner called **The Lusitania** was struck by Germany. America had ammo and guns on the ship, and they sank it. They were trying to get America to stop sending guns and ammo to their enemy.

The next thing that happened was that Germany sent a **telegram** (a note) to Mexico. It said that if Mexico would declare war on America that they would give them all the Mexican Cession land back to them. Remember the Mexican Cession land? Mexico gave it to America to stop the Mexican / American War. This telegram that Germany sent to Mexico was called **The Zimmerman Note**.

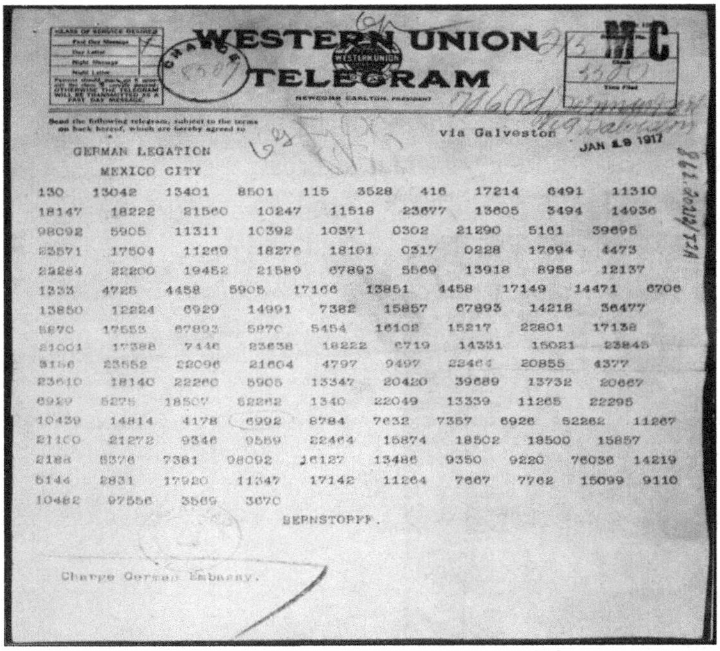
WESTERN UNION TELEGRAM

via Galveston JAN 19 1917

GERMAN LEGATION
MEXICO CITY

130 13042 13401 8501 115 3528 416 17214 6491 11310
18147 18222 21560 10247 11518 23677 13605 3494 14936
98092 5905 11311 10392 10371 0302 21290 5161 39695
23571 17504 11269 18276 18101 0317 0228 17694 4473
22284 22200 19452 21589 67893 5569 13918 8958 12137
1333 4725 4458 5905 17166 13851 4458 17149 14471 6706
13850 12224 6929 14991 7382 15857 67893 14218 36477
5870 17553 67893 5870 5454 16102 15217 22801 17138
21001 17388 7446 23638 18222 6719 14331 15021 23845
3156 23552 22096 21604 4797 9497 22464 20855 4377
23610 18140 22260 5905 13347 20420 39689 13732 20667
6929 5275 18507 52262 1340 22049 13339 11265 22295
10439 14814 4178 6992 8784 7632 7357 6926 52262 11267
21100 21272 9346 9559 22464 15874 18502 18500 15857
2188 5376 7381 98092 16127 13486 9350 9220 76036 14219
5144 2831 17920 11347 17142 11264 7667 7762 15099 9110
10482 97556 3569 3670

BERNSTORFF.

Charge German Embassy.

Zimmerman Note

Figure 53

Germany also started something called **unrestricted submarine warfare.** This was when they would attack and sink every ship that came into the Atlantic Ocean. Once this happened, America got involved in this war. **Woodrow Wilson** was the President at the time, and he didn't want to get involved, but he said that America needed to make the world a safe place for **democracy.** (elected representatives in a country to represent the people). *Remember: Woodrow Wilson's foreign policy was all about morals.* He wanted to make the world a better place for democracy, so this fit with his beliefs.

Before America got involved in this war, which is known as **World War I**, there was talk and the spreading of news about the war and why America needed to get involved. This talk and news is called **propaganda**.

In order for Americans to want to support the war the message needed to be spread that there would be a need for nurses, soldiers, sailors, and support of the American people. Wilson also started the **Selective Service Act** in 1917. This said that if you were a male and age 18, you had to go to war.

The propaganda was a series of posters and news to get the American people to support the war. The American government wanted people to buy **war bonds** with their money. If a person was not actually participating in the war, they could help by purchasing war bonds and the government will use the money to fight the war. When the war was over, they would get their money back plus interest.

Figure 54   Propaganda

Americans were also encouraged to **conserve resources.** This meant that no one should waste any food, meat, bread, milk, etc. because that food needed to go to the soldiers.

NOTES:

Figure 55

The other thing that needed to happen to convince the American people to go to war was to **dehumanize** the enemy. This was when the propaganda tried to convince people that anything from Germany was bad.

Figure 56

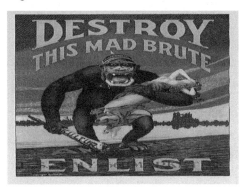

Posters that promoted protesting of the war were not allowed! Only posters about conserving food, eating less, planting gardens, saving money, and buying more war bonds, and being afraid of the enemy - German, were allowed.

There was even a law that said if an American was caught talking bad about the war they could be thrown in jail. This was called **The Espionage and Sedition Act**. It violated the American people's Freedom of Speech, but it happened.

Some of the names of German things were even changed because it was considered a crime in the United States to speak the German language, or even to teach German. For example, the word *frankfurter* was changed to *hot dog* because this was a German word.

Questions:

1.   What were the alliances in Europe? Name the countries.

2.   Why did a war break out in Europe?

3.   In the beginning, how was America involved? What did they do?

4.   What did Germany do that made things more intense for America?

5.   What was unrestricted submarine warfare?

6.   Why did Woodrow Wilson think we should get involved in WWI?

7.   What three main points did the war propaganda try to make?

8.   How did war bonds work?

9.   Why would the American people be reluctant to get involved in a war in Europe at this time, if you had to guess? Explain.

WRITE!

Imagine you were a young soldier being sent to fight in a war you knew little about. Write a letter home to your family about your feelings and anxieties.

Imagine you were a young child or mother staying home while your father or husband went to fight in a war you knew little about. Write a letter to your father or husband explaining what is happening at home.

Lesson 4.5: War is Hard and Expensive

Once America got involved in World War I, they started to see just how bad it really was. People had cameras and they could take pictures of how bad everything was. Americans started to feel that all the propaganda they were supposed to believe in and to support was not how it really was. Americans started to feel the need to isolate themselves and stay out of problems with foreign countries.

When the war was over a peace negotiation was held in Versailles, France. This was called **THE VERSAILLES CONFERENCE, 1919**. No one really won this war. A peace treaty was signed to stop the fighting.

Woodrow Wilson was still President, and even though the war was over, he wanted to continue to try to spread democracy throughout the world. He wanted the United States to get involved in **The League of Nations.** This was when countries formed together to meet and discuss ways to try to avoid future wars. America attended some of the meetings, but they never joined. What Wilson wanted was a **collective security**, which was where countries would work together to protect one another. He proposed this idea to the Senate, but they voted against it.

Figure 57

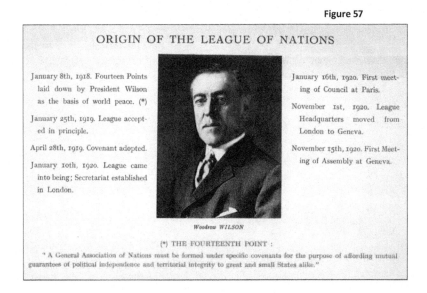

The next President was Warren G. Harding. He promised Americans that he would keep them out of problems with foreign countries. He did get involved with Latin America, but only to make money. He avoided getting involved in their problems or their politics.

Doing business with Latin America was called **The Good Neighbor Policy**. Another thing Warren G. Harding accomplished was loaning money to Germany to help them pay for their debt from World War I. This was known as the **Dawes and Young Plans**.

Meanwhile, in Germany a man named **Adolph Hitler** was slowly becoming a dictator and a man named **Mussolini** was doing the same thing in Italy. The American Congress found some new information that there had been some things that were sneaky which pushed America into World War I. Some Americans became so angry about this that they pushed for **Neutrality Acts** which would keep them out of any foreign wars in the future.

Figure 58

Questions:

1. Who won World War I?
2. How did war make Americans feel?

3. What was the peace negotiation to end the war called?
4. What was The League of Nations and collective security?

5. What did Warren G. Harding do about foreign countries?

6. What were the Dawes and Young Plans?

7. Who were the two dictators that were emerging in Europe after World War I?

8. What were the neutrality acts?

RESEARCH!

Spend some time researching the lives of emerging dictators introduced in this section. Take some notes and create a short presentation of interesting facts about them. Share with a classmate.

Lesson 4.6: Modern America:
1920-1930 BOOM!

World War I was over, and Americans were moving away from wanting imperialism (conquering other countries). They wanted things *back to normal*, and they started to isolate themselves. Everything was about "America first". The economy was booming, and Henry Ford's invention of the assembly line meant that products were being produced very quickly.

Figure 59

An assembly line

People wanted to buy things to make life easier, more modern. Everybody wanted a radio, and many were able to buy one. This was a big deal. Having radios in the home meant the entertainment industry started to grow in popularity.

Another thing that everyone wanted was appliances. The assembly line helped make appliances readily available and the **installment plans** made everything affordable by making it possible for people to make monthly payments to make large purchases. Remember the **Great Migration**? This was when the African Americans from the south started to move into the cities to find work. This occurred between 1916-1930. There was so much racism in the south during this time. The KKK was a hate group against anything other than them.

There were 5 million members of the KKK during this time and they spread hate and terror against anyone who supported anything to do with black people or any race other than white.

In the 1920's, some Americans believed that the only people that should be living in the United States were the people who were actually born there. They developed a fear of foreigners called **xenophobia.**

Americans became very sensitive to anything to do with Russia, called **The Bolshevik Revolution**. Eastern European people or ideas were also rejected during this time. Americans wanted to stay away from anyone who was suspected of being communist, socialist, or an anarchist.

Laws started to reduce how many people immigrated into the United States. There was something called the First **red scare**, which was the fear of communism taking over the United States. The American people wanted the attorney general to find all the communists living in America and kick them out. This was called **The Palmer Raids** because **Mitchell Palmer** was the attorney general at this time. Hundreds and thousands of people were deported because of this.

America placed immigration quotas on people coming from Southern or Eastern Europe. This meant there were only a certain number of people allowed to come to America from these countries.

There was a national case called **Sacco and Vanzetti Trial**. Italian immigrants named Sacco and Vanzetti were arrested for murder and were executed on evidence that wasn't really believable at all.

Figure 60

110

Another thing that happened was a substitute teacher in Tennessee was found to be teaching **evolution** to students (the belief that people evolved from apes). The teacher, named John Scopes, was put on trial for doing this because it was against Christianity. This was called **The Scopes Monkey Trial**, and it was a big deal at this time.

The belief in evolution is called **Darwinism**, and this went directly against Christianity. A man named **William Jennings Bryan** came in during this time to try to send John Scopes to jail. The **ACLU (American Civil Liberties Union)** came in to defend John Scopes. Mr. Scopes was found guilty, but he only served about a week in prison.

NOTES:

Questions:

1. What invention helped most Americans buy radios and appliances?

2. What is an installment plan?

3. What is the term for "fear of foreigners?"

4. What was the red scare?

5. We arrested people who were suspected of being communists. What was this called?

6. What was an immigration quota?

7. What happened to Sacco and Vanzetti?

8. How many members of the KKK were active during this time?

9. Who was John Scopes, and what was his crime?

10. What one invention gave the entertainment industry a boost?

WRITE!

Think about the installment plans and make a list of pros and cons for taking advantage of them to buy things. Make another list of products you think should be purchased on an installment plan and products that should not be purchased on an installment plan. State your reasons why you believe this.

Lesson 4.7: Women, African Americans, & Organized Crime

Women in the 1920s-1930s were being attacked. They were expected to be in the kitchen and having children, but many women wanted something different. They wanted to be able to get out of the house, vote, and work! Women started to go out to clubs, dressing sexy and dancing. They were drinking alcohol, smoking, and having a good time outside of the home for the first time. The men were worried about this change. There was something called **The Temperance Movement** that said the alcohol was causing problems.

Figure 61

A daring outfit for a woman in 1920s-1930s America.

The Harlem Renaissance was a time in America in New York when African Americans had a great influence on anything considered intellectual. They were writing novels, poetry, composing art and music. Their published works were being integrated into the schools. Black music was becoming hugely popular in America, and everyone loved the new sound. People were listening to it on their radios and enjoying this new type of music and live performances by black musicians was great entertainment at the clubs.

Figure 62

Because people considered alcohol to be causing too much partying and change at this time, the **18th amendment** was written which prohibited the sale and consumption of alcoholic beverages in the United States. This period in time was called **Prohibition**.

This sudden change of law caused all the partying to stop until someone named **Al Capone** started a group of people to sneak alcohol into the clubs and cities. They did this by hiding alcohol in the side of their boots and then walking into the clubs to distribute it. This group of people were known as "gangsters" or **organized crime.** The practice of bringing in alcohol was called **bootlegging** because they hid the alcohol in their boots! Organized crime became huge during Prohibition, and soon alcohol was being brought in on a regular basis in much larger quantities.

Speakeasies became a popular way to break the 18th amendment. These were secret places to go party and drink alcohol. People had to have a secret word or phrase to get in. There would be a small door in a hidden place. A person would knock on the door in a certain way, and someone would open another smaller door and ask for the secret word. The code must be spoken softly so no one would hear.

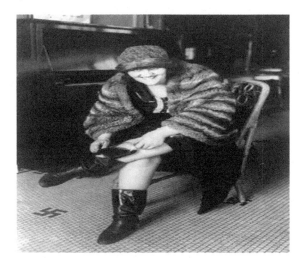

A bootlegger during Prohibition.   **Figure 63**

If the code was correct, the door was open and inside was dancing, drinking, and fun. Soon, America realized that the 18th amendment wasn't working and only creating more crime. The organized crime gangs were really growing and starting to take over the cities. The **21st amendment** was eventually passed, which overturned the 18th amendment. It allowed alcohol to become legal once again.

Questions:

1.   What was the big change with women during this time period?

2.   What was the Harlem Renaissance, and where was it located? Explain.

3.   What was the temperance movement?
4.   What was the 18th amendment?

5.   What was organized crime, and what "crime" did they commit?

6.   Who was the leader of organized crime in New York?

7.   How did bootlegging get its name? Explain.

8.   What was a speakeasy? Explain.

9.   What was the 21st amendment?

10.   What is another name for the time period when drinking or selling alcohol was illegal in America?

PROJECT!

Imagine you are living in the time of Prohibition. Write a short play depicting a weekend in the life of a young adult during this time. Be sure to include things you've learned in this section. Act the play out with your friends.

Lesson 4.8: The Economy Crashes: BUST!

Remember the installment plans? Well, Americans were buying things they couldn't really afford, and making payments monthly through the installment plans the banks were offering. The Federal Reserve lowered the interest rate so low that anybody could buy anything they wanted because it was so easy to get approval - whether they could afford it or not!

Some people wanted to buy stock and invest in companies, but didn't have any money to buy stocks, so what did they do? They borrowed money from the bank to buy stock. This was called **buying on speculation** because nobody knew if the stocks would make money or not.

When the stock would lose money, the person who borrowed the money from the bank couldn't pay the bank back. This happened too many times and created a problem where the whole nation was in economic trouble.

The banks were losing so much money in the late 1920s because of this. Eventually, the banks ran out of money and the stock market CRASHED meaning there were no more stocks to buy and no more money at the bank. At the same time this happened, the farming economy crashed because there was a decline in crop production called **The Dust Bowl**.

Figure 64

The Dust Bowl

This was a time when there was little to no rain and severe dust storms caused people to lose their farms and way of life. They started to migrate West to try to farm. They traveled on **Route 66**, which was a famous road taking them from the Midwest to the West coast.

Herbert Hoover was the President during this time. He tried increasing taxes to generate money from the wealthy. This did not work. He also created a tariff to stop trading with outside countries, but this only led to the overproduction of goods.

He wanted to avoid a system of **direct relief** or **welfare** where the government gave people money. He did not want people to be dependent on the government for money. Many Americans lived in tight quarters in houses that were barely standing called a **shanty**. Some called these neighborhoods **Shantytown and Hooverville**.

All these factors contributed to **The Great Depression**, a time period in America of great loss and suffering. During this time, many people who were once rich had nothing. Many people lost their homes and many starved. The Veterans of World War I could not get their payments. They marched on Washington, D.C. to try to get their money, but this didn't work. People were angry and wanted a new leadership in America.

Questions:

1. How did the installment plans lead to economic problems? Explain.

2. What did the Federal Reserve do to attract more people to borrow money?

3. What was buying on speculation? Explain.

4. What happened to the farmers during this same time period?

5. When farmers lost everything, where did they go?
6. What was the famous road that farmers used to go west?
7. What was considered direct relief or welfare?

8. What were the tiny houses and neighborhoods called?
9. What was this time period known as?

10. What did the Veterans of World War I want, but could not get?

RESEARCH!

Search for interesting stories and people affected by The Great Depression. Write a short narrative explaining what you learned and share it with a friend.

Lesson 4.9: New Leadership

The former Governor of New York, **Franklin Delano Roosevelt (FDR)** became the next President. He had the difficult job of pulling America out of The Great Depression. He came up with a plan called the three R's: Relief, Recovery, and Reform. He said, *"the only thing we have to fear is fear itself."*

Figure 65

FDR

He created a bank holiday where all the banks closed so he could look at the situation more closely. He went on the radio and talked to the American people every night to give them reassurance that everything would be okay. This program was called **fireside chats** and it would come on in the evenings.

He created something called **The New Deal**. He created many, many corporations that had abbreviations for names. These corporations became known as "alphabet soup" because of the abbreviations. (Examples: FDIC, NRA, AAA)

One of the corporations was the **FDIC (Federal Deposit Insurance Corporation)**. This encouraged Americans to deposit their money into the bank because it guaranteed that if the economy crashed that the government would make sure their money was still there.

Another corporation was the **AAA (Agricultural Adjustment Administration).** This program gave the farmers money to live and asked them to take a break from farming. This allowed the supply to decrease which meant the prices could go up for what they had.

The **NRA (National Recovery Administration)** was another corporation that gave everyone a fair competition to give everyone a fair chance to make a good living whether they had lots of money or not. The **SEC (Securities and Exchange Commission)** regulated the stock market and penalized those that were cheating.

Franklin D. Roosevelt got people back to work and making money by creating the **CCC (Civilian Conservation Corps)** which gave people jobs building and working in the National Parks across America.

The **Public Works Administration** gave people jobs building roads, dams, and sewage systems for cities. The **TVA (Tennessee Valley Authority)** put people to work making electricity available to people living in remote areas in Tennessee. The **Social Security Act** gave elderly people insurance and a monthly salary that they could live on without working.

It is not necessary to memorize all these corporations - the main thing is that you understand that Franklin Delano Roosevelt got people in America back to work and working fairly. He got money back in the banks and restored the trust of many.

Some people did not like the New Deal. Some people even tried to sue him. An example of this was a group of chicken farmers tried to sue him. In the Supreme Court case named **Schechter Poultry Company v. US**, these chicken farmers sued the government for trying to make them stop farming and just take money. The Supreme Court ruled that the **NRA (National Recovery Administration)** was unconstitutional.

FDR was elected to a second term and had the support of many Americans. His New Deal did not bring America out of the Great Depression, but it did provide relief for people who were suffering.

NOTES:

Questions:

1. What was known as the 3 r's?

2. What was Franklin Delano Roosevelt (FDR) known for saying?

3. What was the fireside chat?

4. What was the New Deal? Explain.

5. What was alphabet soup?

6. Give two examples of how FDR put people back to work.

7. How did FDR get people to put their money in the banks again?

8. How did FDR protect the elderly who could not work anymore?

9. Why did the chicken farmers sue the government?

10. Did FDR's New Deal end the Great Depression?

RESEARCH/PROJECT!

Use a search engine to listen to some of FDR's famous speeches and fireside chats. Take some notes about what you hear and create a short slide presentation or movie to show how he helped to calm America down during this time of crisis.

Lesson 4.9 (A): Dictators

America was recovering from the many economic problems they experienced with The Great Depression. In the rest of the world, there were dictators taking over certain countries. **Joseph Stalin** was the dictator of **The Soviet Union**. **Benito Mussolini** was the dictator of **Italy**. **Adolph Hitler** was the dictator of **Germany**. **Hideki Tojo** was the dictator of **Japan**. Remember, a dictator is a person that controls a country in which there is no voting system.

Figure 66 & 67

Joseph Stalin, dictator of The Soviet Union

Benito Mussolini, dictator of Italy

Figure 68

Adolph Hitler, dictator of Germany

Hideki Tojo, dictator of Japan

Figure 69

America knew that the dictators were expanding and trying to gain more control, but they were not getting involved because of the problems that were going on with the economy at that time. Japan was trying to take Hawaii, The Philippines, and Guam away from America. At this same time, Germany was secretly building a military. Both countries were doing things that *threatened* to go to war. This is called **militarism.**

Because America did not want to go to war or get involved with foreign countries, they practiced something called **appeasement**. This means that America was talking nicely with foreign countries about what was going on. In other words, fighting and physical contact was not happening. The result of this appeasement was not good. For example, America told Germany not to invade Poland but Hitler (the dictator of Germany) did it anyway in 1939. America was trying to keep the world from going to war.

When Germany invaded Poland, Britain and France declared war on Germany. This was because of the alliance system where countries partner together to help each other out. When this happened, The Soviet Union and America remained neutral (they did not take sides). Germany was practicing a new type of warfare called **Blitzkrieg**. This is when the enemy is taken lightning fast, by surprise. They also were using **Panzer Tanks** to "blitz" Poland and France before they even knew what was happening!

Britain and France were defeated but America remained neutral. America was in **isolationism** mode, which meant they did not want to get involved with other countries.

Questions:

1. What is a dictator?

2. Why did America want to remain neutral even though there were dictators threatening war on other countries?

3. What did Japan want from America?

4. What is the alliance system?

5.   How was Germany fighting in a very different way than had ever happened before?

6.   What is it called when a country talks nicely to another country to try to avoid going to war?

7.   What is isolationism?

WRITE!

In your journal, write about what you have learned about the benefits of isolationism versus imperialism. Should America get involved with other countries or not? Why do you believe this?

Lesson 4.9 (B): America Gets Involved in WWII

Figure 70

FDR and his involvement in World War II.

America wanted to help with the problems in Europe but did not want to get directly involved in the conflict. They did this by sending aid to some of the countries. This was called **Neutrality Acts.** America said that they would give them **The Arsenal of Democracy,** which was guns, weapons, destroyers, and use of our naval bases. There was something called **Cash and Carry** in 1939 that allowed other countries to pay America to use their guns, but they had to come to America to get them.

Another way that America got involved in the war is through the **Destroyers for Bases** plan in 1940. America gave Britain destroyers (ships) in return for naval bases. The **Lend Lease Act** of 1941 was where another country could borrow America's entire arsenal of war (military equipment) because it was not being used at the time.

And remember learning about the **draft**? This was a system in America where when a young man turns 18, he is automatically signed up to be a soldier for the United States military if needed. FDR (Franklin D. Roosevelt) created a **Peacetime Draft**. This was his way of bringing back the draft system. Because he wanted to reassure the American people that they were not getting involved in any wars, he called it a peacetime draft. He also made the promise that America's young men would not be sent to any foreign wars.

FDR signed the Peacetime Draft and promised that no young men would be fighting in any foreign wars.

What happened next got America involved in World War II. So, Japan was getting really close to Hawaii and Pearl Harbor. They were threatening to take it. America responded by putting an **embargo** on all the American oil that was being sold to Japan. This means they stopped selling oil to Japan. Japan responded to this embargo by sending planes to Pearl Harbor and they attacked the naval base there on December 7, 1941. America declared war on Japan the very next day.

Figure 71

Japan attacks America's naval base on Pearl Harbor, Hawaii. America declares war on Japan the very next day.

There were two sides to this war. **The Axis Pact:** Japan, Italy, and Germany. The other side was called **The Allies**. This was Britain, Soviet Union, and America.

The **propaganda** of war started to happen again to get the American people to support this war effort, just like what happened in WWI.

Questions:

1.   What was the Arsenal of Democracy?

2.   What types of programs did America have that allowed Britain to use their weapons and supplies?

3.   What is the draft?

4.   What did FDR promise to the American people?

5. What event led America to declare war on Japan?

6. What were the two sides of the war named? What countries were on each side?

7. What is propaganda?

8. How did America try to stop Japan from taking Pearl Harbor in Hawaii?

RESEARCH!

Look at some of the propaganda posters from the World War II era. What common themes do you see? Create a visual representation of your favorite World War II propaganda posters and be able to explain what message they were trying to convey.

Lesson 4.9 (C): The Goals of WWII Propaganda

As you learned in the last section, America declared war on Japan the day after Japan attacked Pearl Harbor, America's naval base in Hawaii. To gain the support of the American people, **propaganda** was created to influence their thoughts and actions. The goals of that propaganda were *shut up, produce, sacrifice, and hate.*

SHUT UP: This propaganda suggested that women talked too much. They were gossiping about the war. The government wanted to send the message that women needed to stop talking about the war because there could be spies walking around listening to the talk. The women were supposed to keep their mouths shut about where in the world their husbands were concerning the war or their involvement in the war. The propaganda suggested that women gossiping could result in their husbands being killed.

Figure 72   Propaganda

SHUT YOUR EARS: This propaganda also suggested for people to NOT LISTEN to the Germans. The German propaganda was trying to influence Americans to be on their side in the war. The American government wanted the people to stay away from anything German.

PRODUCE: This propaganda called for American workers to NOT STRIKE during wartime. All of the workforce was supposed to be working daily to produce guns, ammo, uniforms, and anything else needed to support the war. America created **The War Production Board** where any factory in America was changed into a gun/ammunition/war factory producing goods for the war.

Figure 73   Promoting the War

WOMEN PRODUCING: This propaganda convinced America that women should be working in the factories to help. Also, no discrimination would happen based on race or ethnicity during wartime. Everyone would get a job.

Figure 74

This is *Rosie the Riveter*. She works in factories to produce war supplies, encouraging women to work "like a man".

SACRIFICE: Restrictions were placed on the American people. They gave people something called **rations**. This was a set amount of product that each family could purchase each week. For example, one family may only be allowed to purchase one loaf of bread each week during wartime. **The Office of Price Administration** made sure that prices did not go up during this time, and the American family was given a **ration book** that showed how much food/product they were using each week. The money that was not being spent on food should be spent on buying **war bonds** to support the war.

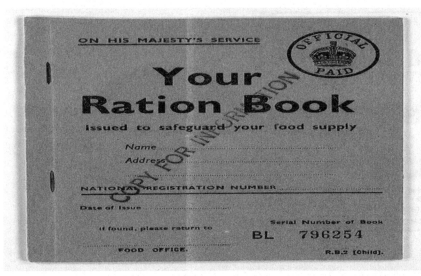

A ration book   **Figure 75**

Use this space to take notes and make a list of some of the things that were rationed. THINK: What would be rationed if this happened today?

HATE: Finally, the World War II propaganda focused on convincing America to hate the enemy: Germany and Japan. America took the Japanese people that were living in the United States and placed them in camps. They were treated badly. Their homes were taken away from them. They lost everything they had built and worked for. Anything German was considered wrong and bad. The German language was no longer taught in schools. German words such as *frankfurter* were changed to different words such as *hot dog* because people were not supposed to use anything German.

Figure 76

As you can see, the propaganda started again to convince the American people to support the war. The German and Japanese immigrants were suddenly not accepted. Later, a Japanese American man named *Korematsu* filed a lawsuit against the United States for taking away all he had worked for. He was actually born in America and had only lived in America his entire life. He won that case named **Korematsu v. United States.** Much later in history when Ronald Reagan was President, he signed a bill that gave the Japanese Americans money for everything they went through during World War II. This money was called **reparations.**

NOTES:

Figure 77

Questions:

1.   What were the main goals of World War II propaganda?

2.   What was a ration? Explain the ration book.

3.   Who were Americans supposed to hate?

4.   What was the *shut up, shut your ears* propaganda? Explain.

5.   What did *Rosie the Riveter* represent? Explain.

6.   What happened to the factories in America?

7.   What were Americans supposed to do with the money they were saving on not buying too many groceries and products?

8.   What happened to the Japanese Americans during this time?

9. Why did Korematsu win his case against the United States?

10. What did Ronald Reagan do for the Japanese?

PROJECT!

Use a search engine to discover images of ration books from World War II. Create a ration book for modern day society. What would it look like? Why would the things you chose need to be rationed in this day and time period?

Lesson 4.9 (D):   World War II

World War II was a **total war**. This means that America was completely and totally involved in this war. The most powerful people leading the war were known as **the big 3.** They were **Winston Churchill of Britain, Franklin D. Roosevelt of America, and Joseph Stalin of The Soviet Union (Russia).**

The Big 3

Figure 78

There was a meeting of the big 3 called **The Yalta Conference.** This is where they tried to decide what they were going to do with Europe after they defeated Germany. They decided that The Soviet Union (Russia), would get part of Germany and some of the other countries in Europe would get the rest of Germany. This conference was held in February of 1945.

They also decided to create a **United Nations** type of group where all the world was against dictators (one ruler over all the people). It is true that Joseph Stalin of Russia was a dictator, but he agreed because they all needed to work together to defeat Germany. A famous saying at this time was, *the enemy of my enemy is my friend.* Joseph Stalin did want to help Russia before attacking Germany, but America did not do this. Stalin would not ever forget this.

136

The first war strategy was called **Europe First**. This meant that The Allied Powers dealt with Europe first. This part of the war became known as **The European Theater**. Britain was helped first. In **Operation Torch**, America and Britain started attacking German forces in North Africa. **George Patton**, a famous American General was known for the successful operation.

General George Patton

Figure 79

Next, Italy was invaded, and dictator Mussolini was overthrown from power. This was in 1943. Meanwhile, Russia was still getting attacked by Germany and Stalin was upset with America for not helping Russia more. The next country the Allied forces invaded was France.

NOTES:

Germany had occupied this country, and Allied troops invaded Normandy, France on June 6, 1944 in what is known as **D- Day**. The troops came in off the water and invaded land in France. The troops faced cannons, machine guns, snipers, and if they survived, they were lucky.
This was a horrible massacre.

Figure 80   D-Day

Questions:

1. Who were the Big 3?

2. At the conference, what was the main objective?

3. Why did Joseph Stalin agree to rid the world of dictators when he himself was one?

4. What was the European Theater? Explain.

5. Why was Joseph Stalin angry with America?

6. Where was Operation Torch? Was it successful?

7. What type of invasion was used to attack France?

8. What was the name of the famous invasion of France?

9. Why were the troops so easily killed during this invasion?

10. What does the saying, *the enemy of my enemy is my friend*, mean? Explain.

WRITE!

Think about warfare and strategy. In your opinion, was D-Day a good war strategy? Why or why not? If you do not know enough about D-Day, spend some time researching it online and looking at images before you write your opinion.

Lesson 4.9 (E):   World War II Continues

After D-Day, many soldiers were killed. Remember, this was when Allied soldiers landed in Normandy, France by sea. Even though many soldiers were dead, Germany saw that France had been invaded and they started to push back. This *pushing back* looked like a straight line of German soldiers pushing the American soldiers back, away from France. This created a bulge. A bulge is like a straight line being turned into a curved line, like a fat belly sticking out over pants. Because of the bulge the soldiers created, this battle was called **The Battle of the Bulge.**

The **Tuskegee Airmen** were a group of black fighter pilots in America. They took Germany and conquered France, and this is how America conquered Europe. This was called **V-E Day (Victory in Europe)** and it happened on May 8, 1945.

Figure 81

A member of the Tuskegee Airmen smiling next to his plane.

Now that Europe had been conquered, the Allied Forces had to deal with Japan. Japan had already taken over a naval base in the Philippines. The Allied Forces needed a plan to attack Japan. Remember: Japan is an island. So, the **Island-Hopping Campaign** was the plan to take over smaller islands surrounding Japan to use as landing strips for fighter planes. Japan is in the Pacific Ocean, so this part of World War II was called **The Pacific Theater.** (look at the map on the next page).

Figure 82

From June 4-7 the Allied Forces got the Philippines back from Japan in the **Battle of Midway**. This was an island between America and Japan, that is why it was called the Battle of Midway. This was a naval battle, and it was a big victory for the Allies. Other battles were **The Battle of Iwo Jima** and **the Battle of Okinawa**. The Allies were getting closer and closer to Japan with each battle, but the Japanese were not giving up.

The Japanese military actually ran out of ammunition. They had nothing to fight with. So, what they did was fly fighter planes into Allied troops and ships, killing the pilot. These pilots were called **Kamikaze** pilots.

Questions:

1.   Explain the Battle of the Bulge.

2.   What group was responsible for winning the war in Europe? What was this day called?

3.   What strategy did Allied forces design to attack Japan?

4.   What was the name of the second part of World War II when Allied Forces went after Japan?

5.   What happened when Japan ran out of ammunition to fight?

WRITE!

In your journal, write about the Japanese military. What did they do that surprised you? What did they do that impressed you, if anything? What did they do that angered you? Express your thoughts through your writing, free style.

PROJECT!

In your journal, draw a map of The Battle of the Bulge to help you remember.

Lesson 4.9 (F): The Atomic Bombs & The Effects

As you have learned, Japan would not give up or surrender. Harry S. Truman was the United States President during this time. He decided that no more men would die in this war. He didn't want any more American lives lost. America had an **atomic bomb**, which is a nuclear weapon capable of destroying an entire country.

Truman called a meeting known as **The Potsdam Conference** where he had Winston Churchill, Joseph Stalin, and some other leaders together to make this decision. A letter was sent to Japan informing them that if they did not surrender, they would be destroyed.

The first bomb that was dropped on Japan was called **Little Boy. Paul Tibbets** is the name of the pilot that flew the plane and dropped this atomic bomb on Japan. The name of his plane was **The Enola Gay.** This first atomic bomb was dropped on Hiroshima. This happened on August 6, 1945.

Figure 83

On August 9, 1945, a second atomic bomb called **Fat Boy** was dropped on Nagasaki. After this, Japan surrendered, and the war was over. The surrender was on September 2, 1945. One bomb killed over 100,000 people and caused massive destruction. America gave Japan money to rebuild after the surrender, and Japan allied with the United States.

Because of the dropping of two atomic bombs, America became known as a *superpower*, and the best country in the world. As a result of the war effort with the building of bombs, tanks, and the production of ammunition, the United States economy was doing great. This is because so many people were working, producing, and they were also conserving money for the war.

Interestingly, from the science that created the nuclear or atomic bomb, it was discovered how to create heat. This led to the invention of the microwave oven.

Figure 84

Questions:

1.   How was the decision made to drop the atomic bomb on Japan? Explain.

2.   How many bombs were dropped on Japan?

3.   Did anything good come from the dropping of the atomic bombs? Explain why you think this.

4.   Why do you think that no more atomic bombs have been dropped since World War II?

WRITE!

In your journal, write down your thoughts about being the President of the United States during this time of war. What are the challenges? What are the anxieties? What do you think Harry Truman's life was like during this time? Allow your thoughts to move freely from your mind to your journal.

Lesson 4.9 (G): Germany's Hatred Towards Jewish People

It was discovered that before and after World War II, Adolph Hitler, dictator of Germany, blamed the Jewish people for all of Germany's problems. He hated Jewish people. He created something called **The Nuremberg Laws** in 1935. These laws allowed a political group called the **Nazis**, to commit horrible crimes against Jewish people. Who were the Nazis? They were a group of people that supported Adolph Hitler and his ideas.

One example of what the Nazis did was gathering Jewish people together and taking them to places called **Concentration Camps**. Once in the camp the person would be stripped, beaten, starved, tortured, and killed. Some were killed by starvation, others were killed using lethal gas, and others were shot. Their bodies were buried in mass graves.

These terrible acts are considered **Crimes Against Humanity**, **the Holocaust**, **Genocide**, or sometimes called **A Final Solution**. **Kristallnacht** was a night when the Nazis burned and destroyed everything that the Jewish people had, and many were killed in the street. In English, Kristallnacht means *night of broken glass*. Sadly, 11 million Jewish people and others were killed before anyone did anything about it.

Concentration Camp in Germany.   **Figure 85**

Later, in the United States, trials were held for the Nazis that participated in these crimes of humanity during the Holocaust. 12 Nazis were judged for their crimes and given the death penalty by the United States Courts. This was known as **The Nuremberg Trials.**

Another thing the United States government did was to give the remaining Jewish people a new home. All the governments in the world came together and took land from Palestine. They called this land **Israel**, and they gave it to the Jewish people to live in a new land. Today, the Palestine people and the Israeli people fight over this land, and Israel is closely allied with the United States.

Figure 86

NOTES:

Questions:

1.   Why did Hitler hate the Jewish people?

2.   What is Kristallnacht?

3.   What is a concentration camp?

4.   What did the United States do to punish the Nazis for their crimes?

5.   What is a Nazi?

6.   How did the nations around the world give the Jewish people a new place to live?

7.   How did the Jewish people react to their new land?

8.   How did the Palestinian people react to their land being taken away from them?

9.   What do you think happened to Adolph Hitler?

10. What do you think the phrase, *11 million Jews and others were killed during the holocaust...* refers to? Who do you think *the others* were? Don't be afraid to research this question!

RESEARCH/PROJECT!

After researching question number 10, create a slideshow presentation or movie that explains at least one angle or perspective of the holocaust. This can be anything that you feel compelled to research and then explain.

Unit 5: LEGACY OF THE COLD WAR
Lesson 5.1: Stopping the Spread of Communism

After World War II, America's focus was on *stopping the spread of communism* around the world. America was also concerned with stopping the production of nuclear weapons and bombs. At this time, Russia and America both had nuclear power. America was worried about Russia having a nuclear bomb and Russia was worried about America having a nuclear bomb. There were many threats between the two countries, but actual combat never happened. This was called **The Cold War**.

To stop the spread of communism throughout the world, **The United Nations** worked together to try to keep peace. This is where many nations come together for a common goal. During this time, communism was in Russia and the goal of The United Nations was to keep that communism from spreading to other countries.

Winston Churchill, leader of Britain said that there was an **iron curtain** falling over the eastern European countries. The iron curtain separated Russian fear (in eastern Europe) from western Europe. The American President was **Harry S. Truman**. He created **The Truman Doctrine** that allowed America to help Greece and Turkey to break away from Russian communism.

Another thing that America did to stop the spread of communism was known as **The Marshall Plan**. This was designed by General George C. Marshall to give money to foreign countries who were close to becoming overtaken by communism.

BERLIN

Berlin is a city in the center of Germany. After World War II, America controlled the western part of Germany (a democracy) and Russia controlled the eastern side of Germany (communist). Berlin was right in the middle of these two sides of Germany, and it was a democracy.

Just after the war there was a spy named **George Keenan**. He found out that the Russians were trying to spread communism to the western part that America controlled. Many Germans tried to escape from communism by heading west to Berlin. The leader of Russia at that time, **Nikita Khrushchev**, had a wall built in Berlin to separate east Germany from west Germany. If people tried to get over the wall they were shot.

The Berlin Wall

Figure 87

Questions:

1.   The Berlin Wall is now removed. Do a mini-research on when this happened and what you
could see today if you were to visit Berlin.

2.   What was America's main goal after World War II?

3.   How was Germany divided after World War II? Explain.

4.   What was the Cold War about?

5.	How did the Marshall Plan help stop the spread of communism?

6.	How did the Truman Doctrine help stop the spread of communism?

7.	What is the iron curtain?

8.	What does the United Nations do?

RESEARCH/PROJECT!

Expand on question number 1 above. Create an itinerary for a trip to Berlin today. Create a slideshow presentation or movie for your class to see.

Lesson 5.2: The Cold War Continues

Now that you know about the Berlin wall and how it divided eastern Germany from western Germany, let's look closely at the people who lived in the middle of the city of Berlin. Russia wanted to try to keep Berlin for themselves. They started by blocking all the roads and railways in Berlin that went to west Berlin. This meant that the people in this area could not get food and supplies to live.

America responded to this by creating the **Berlin Airlift**. This was where America used airplanes to fly into the western side of Berlin to give them food and supplies. Russia knew America was doing this, but no actual conflict took place because both America and Russia did not want to get involved in another war. All of this is part of **The Cold War** between Russia and America. The Berlin Wall became a symbol of the Cold War.

The Cold War Alliances:

The United States and western Europe were together called **NATO** (North Atlantic Treaty Organization). Russia and eastern Europe were called **The Warsaw Pact**. Harry S. Truman, American president during this time, did not want China going to Russia and becoming a communist country. Another country trying to become communist was Korea. The United States tried to stop this from happening and got involved in a war over it. This was called **The Korean War**. America lost this war. Korea became divided into two countries after this: **North Korea** and **South Korea**.

The Cold War continued between Russia and America. Each country had nuclear bombs pointed at each other. This is called **M.A.D. (Mutually Assured Destruction)**. Many people in America built shelters underground to protect themselves in case a nuclear bomb hit. People in America became very paranoid and were afraid of communism. This was during the early 1950s.

NOTES:

Figure 88

A Bomb Shelter

In the 1960s Cuba revolted against the United States after an invasion known as **The Bay of Pigs.** America was trying to overthrow **Fidel Castro**, Cuba's communist leader. **The Bay of Pigs** was the name of the main landing area in Cuba, and after the invasion many referred to it as *The Bay of Pigs Disaster.* Russia tried to help them by sending them nuclear missiles. Cuba aimed these missiles at America in what is known as **The Cuban Missile Crisis.** John F. Kennedy was the president of the United States at this time and he responded by having nuclear missiles sent to Turkey pointed at Russia. Once Russia discovered this, they removed the missiles from Cuba.

Social and Cultural Changes

After World War II there were some social changes that happened in America. The soldiers were coming home from fighting, and they were happy to be home with their wives. Many young soldiers wanted to start families. This resulted in many, many babies being born called **The Baby Boom.**

The G.I. Bill was created to help the returning soldiers go to college and take care of their families. This was money sent directly to the soldiers for them to pay for college and to find jobs. This helped them to adjust to life after the war.

When Dwight D. Eisenhower was the president who was responsible for creating the **interstate system**, which is a group of roads and highways that connect the states together in America. He did this to ensure that America could move its military up and down these roads easily to move supplies and weapons around if an attack ever happened. It also encouraged people to move out of the larger cities and into smaller towns nearby, called **suburbs.** People could live in the suburbs and **commute** (travel) to work in the big city by using the interstate highway. This was known as **White Flight** during the Civil Rights Movement.

Women who had worked in the factories during the war wanted to continue working after the war was over. This was the start of more women in the workforce, women as leaders, and women becoming more independent.

People were enjoying a great economy after the war. Vaccines were also being developed and manufactured quickly, resulting in longer life for people and healthier living. Some agricultural changes after the war were that pesticides were being used on crops to kill insects. This technology was used in the war for different reasons, but in some ways helped after the war to keep the crops growing strong.

Questions:

1.   What was the Berlin Airlift? Why was it necessary?

2.   What symbolized the Cold War?

3.   What were the two alliances in the Cold War?

4.   Why did America get involved in The Korean War?

5.   Explain how Russia and the United States threatened each other during the Cold War.

6.   How did the American people react during the threat of nuclear missiles?

7.   What did Russia do to try to help Cuba when they wanted to revolt against the United States?

8.   How did John F. Kennedy stop Cuba from firing the nuclear missiles at The United States?

9.   What was the baby boom?

10.   How did women's roles change after WWII?

11. What were two main changes that happened with the building of the interstate
        highway system in America?

12. Why were people living longer, happier, and healthier lives after World War II? Explain.

WRITE!

In your journal reflect on any positive or negative changes you see in your world today
that could have stemmed from post-World War II.

Lesson 5.3: The Civil Rights Movement

African Americans were beginning to demand what was promised to them - their equal rights. Remember back in Unit 4 when you learned about the Civil War and then the Reconstruction period after the war? The former slaves were promised equal rights. Well, it wasn't happening. Black Americans were still not given the same treatment as white Americans.

There were two main goals of **The Civil Rights Movement**. Equal treatment for African Americans and the right to vote. The Declaration of Independence states that all men are created equal. The Reconstruction Amendments (13th, 14th, and 15th) were in place, but not being enforced at all. African Americans were not allowed their rights!

After World War II was over, African Americans were losing their jobs to white veterans of the war (soldiers coming home from the war). This was happening all over America, both in the North and in the South. The world was watching America, and people were horrified at how badly African Americans were treated. In fact, some foreign countries refused to do business with America because of this.

To fight back against businesses and people that were not giving African Americans equal rights, some protests started. There were **non-violent protests**. An example of this would be when African American customers would peacefully go inside a restaurant and sit in the *whites only* section. (this peaceful protest was called a **sit-in**). They were yelled at, kicked, and had food thrown at them by the owners. Oftentimes, the news media would show up and film and/or photograph everything.

Sometimes, customers would **boycott** a company to hurt their business. This means they would not buy from that company until that company agreed to start treating African American customers the same as white customers.

One famous boycott of the Civil Rights Movement was called **The Montgomery Bus Boycott**. Black American **Rosa Parks** refused to sit in the back of the bus where the African American customers were supposed to sit. She was arrested for this act and shortly after, many people stopped buying tickets for the bus. Many more people supported this peaceful protest until the company changed their policy.

Other famous events of peaceful protests were **Freedom Rides, The March on Washington,** and **The Selma March.** At these events, African Americans were beaten, hosed down with a fire hose, hit with batons, screamed at, and more. People around the world started to take notice.

Dr. Martin Luther King, Jr. gave his famous speech called *I Have a Dream*. This speech spoke to everyone about the fair treatment of all people. **Brown v. The Board of Education** was a famous Supreme Court case in 1954 that stated all public schools shall accept all races of people. This case overturned the **Plessy v. Ferguson** decision to segregate schools.

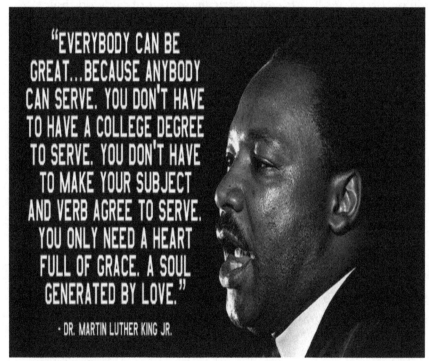

Figure 89

Dr. Martin Luther King, Jr.

The Civil Rights Act of 1964 and **The Voting Rights Act of 1965** ended legal discrimination based on race and overturned the Jim Crow laws at the state level. As a result, voter registration of African Americans in the South increased tremendously. With all the African American voters, things began to change.

Some protests during the Civil Rights Movement were not peaceful. **Malcolm X**, **Stokely Carmichael**, and **The Black Panthers** were groups and leaders who would protest in violent ways. The Hispanic Americans also began to get active about their rights during this time and they led **The Chicano Power**. Women and Native Americans began to get involved in fighting for their equal rights as well.

The **NOW (National Organization for Women)** was a way for women to join and meet to discuss issues facing women's rights in America. **Roe v. Wade** was an important Supreme Court case which ruled that women had the right to have an abortion. This is still a very controversial issue today.

Figure 90   **Women fighting for their rights.**

Questions:

1. What is a sit-in?

2. What is a boycott?

3. What did the African Americans want?

4. What laws in America were failing to protect African Americans?
5. What court case stated that all public schools must be open to all races?

6. What groups and leaders protested in violent ways?

7. What other groups started to fight for their rights?

8. What famous court case stated that a woman has the right to have an abortion?

WRITE!

Option 1: In your journal write a letter from Rosa Parks to one of her family members about her experiences.

Option 2: Listen to Martin Luther King's Speech, *I Have a Dream*. Write to reflect on what you heard.

Option 3: Write a journal reflection on your opinion about Roe v Wade.

Lesson 5.4: John F. Kennedy and Lyndon B. Johnson

John F. Kennedy was the President that was in office during the Cuban Missile Crisis, and he is well-known for that. He also helped society and the people that needed help through a new social program he created known as **The New Frontier**. This program was in support of the Civil Rights Movement. Progression (moving forward) for America was at the center of this program. John F. Kennedy pledged to the American people and to the world that he would put a man on the moon, and that America would be the first to do this. He also started **The Peace Corps**, which was a program where volunteers would travel to foreign countries to promote peace and to help struggling countries with education and building issues.

Vietnam was a focus during this time because the French had lost control of this small country in World War II, and they became vulnerable to becoming communist. Remember, America was interested in stopping the spread of communism. John F. Kennedy got America involved in a war in Vietnam, and he was assassinated shortly after in Dallas, Texas by a man named **Lee Harvey Oswald.** There are many theories as to why he was assassinated, who was involved, and who Lee Harvey Oswald was and why he was motivated to kill the President. These theories are still being debated today.

Figure 91

Vice President, Lyndon B. Johnson becomes President after John F. Kennedy is assassinated.

After John F. Kennedy was assassinated, the vice president, **Lyndon B. Johnson**, took over the presidency. He was responsible for getting **the Voting Rights Act** and **The Civil Rights Act** passed, which ended all voting restrictions that were put in place with the Jim Crow Laws during the Reconstruction era after the Civil War.

The Fair Housing Act of 1968 gave all races of people equal access to housing opportunities in America. The **Affirmative Action Act** gave African Americans equal treatment in terms of job opportunities and programs in public education such as **The Head Start Program,** which enabled pre-school children to attend school for free. He also started **Medicare and Medicaid**, a government funded health care program for the elderly, and he increased **social welfare programs** to assist low-income families with living expenses. He also created more museums with **The National Endowment for Arts & Humanities.** Lyndon B. Johnson called these programs **The Great Society.**

Another thing that he was known for was when he said to the American people that Vietnam attacked American ships at **The Gulf of Tonkin**. This escalated American involvement in the Vietnam War. Later, it was discovered that he lied about this. The American people started to question why they were involved in a foreign war in Vietnam, and protests started to happen against the war. Lyndon B. Johnson did not run for President for another term after this.

Questions:

1. Give some examples of John F. Kennedy's *New Frontier* programs.

2. How did Lyndon B. Johnson become the next president?

3. What is The Peace Corps?

4. Why did America get involved in a war with Vietnam?

5. What were some examples of Lyndon B. Johnson's *Great Society*?

6. What did Lyndon B. Johnson do that made Americans question the war effort in Vietnam?

7. What was the Fair Housing Act?

8. What was Affirmative Action?

9. What is the Head Start program?

10. What is Medicare and Medicaid?

RESEARCH!

Research The New Frontier or The Great Society. What have you learned? Create an infographic, poster, or slideshow presentation showing highlights of your research.

Lesson 5.5: The War in Vietnam

The main purpose for America getting involved with Vietnam is to stop the spread of communism. After World War II, France tried to take over Vietnam because they once owned it and then wanted it back. Vietnam became free from France during World War II. Vietnam wanted to remain an independent country. The Vietnamese leader who fought for their right to be independent was named **Ho Chi Minh.**

Figure 92

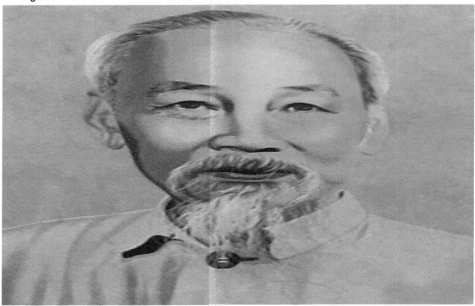

Ho Chi Minh.

North Vietnam was being helped by China, and China was involved with Russia. Ho Chi Minh took the help from the communists because he wanted to be free from France. Because America was trying to stop the spread of communism, they got involved in this war. France was not a communist country, so America sent some people over to Vietnam to help the French. In 1954 at a meeting called **The Geneva Accords**. Vietnam was divided into two parts: North Vietnam (communist) and South Vietnam (not communist). America said that if Vietnam fell into communism, it would be like a domino effect where other countries would follow.

North Vietnam called themselves **The Viet Cong**. America sent troops, money, weapons, and supplies to South Vietnam to fight the Viet Cong. South Vietnam took America's advice and help because they were a superpower. There were some corrupt leaders in South Vietnam at the time, and John F. Kennedy had them assassinated. The Viet Cong depended on supplies from North Vietnam for their success. These supplies came through a trail between two neighboring countries called **Cambodia** and **Laos**. This trail was called **The Ho Chi Minh Trail**. In order to stop the supplies from coming in, Lyndon B. Johnson authorized the bombing of this trail to destroy it in something called **Operation Thunder**.

Figure 93

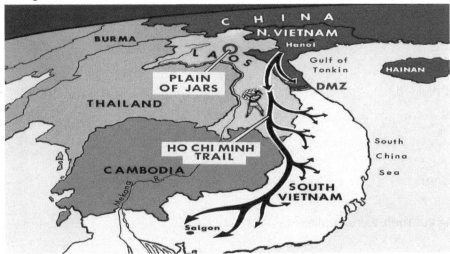

Ho Chi Minh Trail

The American people saw horrible images of the war in Vietnam through news media outlets. They were becoming very angry and started to form opinions about the involvement of Americans in this war. When the soldiers came home from Vietnam, the American people did not see them as heroes, but rather as killers. They were not supported or welcomed home like in past wars. There became a division of people in America called **The Hawks** and **The Doves.** The Hawks were for the war. The doves were against the war. Young men in America were seen burning their draft cards in protest of the war.

In the end, the Viet Cong went on an offensive called **The Tet Offensive**. They attacked anywhere and at any time. American soldiers didn't even know who they were shooting at anymore. There was a loss of life of about 58,000 American soldiers in this war. Shortly after America pulled out of the war, North Vietnam invaded South Vietnam at **Khmer Rouge** and took control.

NOTES:

Questions:

1. What country was trying to take over Vietnam after World War II was over?
2. Who was Ho Chi Minh, and what did he believe?

3. Why did America send troops over to Vietnam?

4. How did Vietnam get divided?

5. What was the Viet Cong?

6. How did the Viet Cong get their war supplies?

7. What did America do to cut off their war supplies?

8. What were young American men doing in protest against the war?

9. What was the Tet offensive?

10. How was America divided in their feelings about the war?

Fun Fact: Shortly after the end of the Vietnam War, the **26th Amendment** was passed making the voting age 18.

RESEARCH!

Use a search engine to research personal stories of people involved in the Vietnam War. Choose your favorite and create a short slideshow presentation to share what you learned.

Lesson 5.6: Richard Nixon's Presidency

There were starting to be many, many protests, and rallies in America during this time about ending American involvement in the Vietnam War. **Richard Nixon** promised the American people that he would pull American troops out of Vietnam if he became President. At **Kent State University**, a college in Ohio, a riot broke out amongst the students about the Vietnam War. The Ohio National Guard had to break it up by coming onto campus with weapons. People were killed.

Meanwhile, in Vietnam, American soldiers were questioning why they were even there. This was called **The Vietnam Cultural Phenomenon.** In order to avoid combat, some soldiers started to bomb the shelters where their commanding officers were staying. This was called **fragging.** In 1973, American soldiers were pulled out of Vietnam. They came home, but they were not welcomed as heroes. Instead, they were treated terribly by most people. They were seen as killers of women and children. There were no welcome parades and there was little respect when they returned.

Figure 94   **Americans protesting the war.**

Nixon tried to get China to be an ally with America and pull away from Russia. This act of trying to be friendly with other countries, by talking and not by force, is called **detente'**. He wanted China to stop supporting North Vietnam. Meanwhile, Vietnam just wanted to be left alone.

They did not want foreign countries interfering in their business. Shortly after American troops were pulled out of Vietnam, during the **Khmer Rouge,** North Vietnam took over South Vietnam. Nixon then had American military attack Cambodia another country close to Vietnam that was vulnerable to communism.

What else did Richard Nixon do during his Presidency? He enforced civil rights laws. He wanted African Americans to be treated equally in America. He also wanted to stop or limit the social welfare programs put in place by Lyndon B. Johnson. He did not want the government to pay for people to live. Something that was important to him was animals and the environment. He passed **The Clean Air and Water Act** and **The Endangered Species Act**. These laws ensured Americans had clean air and safe drinking water. The Endangered Species Act protected animals that were threatened or nearly extinct. He also created the **EPA (the Environmental Protection Agency)**, which was responsible for enforcing laws to protect the environment.

The Pentagon Papers were published during Nixon's presidency. These papers proved that the American government knew that a war would never be won in Vietnam. They proved that the American people had been lied to by the government. This caused people to distrust the government even more (known as the **Credibility Gap**). Finally, Nixon was caught trying to listen to private telephone conversations between the democratic party in what is known as **The Watergate Scandal**. Shortly after this, Richard Nixon resigned from office. He is the only President to date that ever resigned from office.

Richard Nixon resigns.

Figure 95

QUESTIONS:

1. What did Richard Nixon support during his presidency?

2. What did Richard Nixon try to take away during his presidency?

3. What happened at Kent State University?

4. What was happening with the soldiers in Vietnam?

5. Why did Nixon practice 'detente with China?

6. What did Nixon do that made him resign from the presidency?

7. Did President Nixon do anything good in your opinion? Explain.

8. Why was Palestine angry with Israel?

Something to think about:

When a country's focus is on one war, in one part of the world, problems are usually happening in other parts of the world. During Nixon's presidency in the Middle East, there were tensions between Israel and Palestine as a result of America supporting Israel. The Muslim Palestinians did not like the fact that America supported Israel, and new problems were emerging during this time that would develop in the future.

WRITE!

Think about the negative things we think of when we remember President Nixon. Write in your journal about some of these things as well as some of the positive things he did. Why do you think people focus sometimes more on the negative rather than to remember the positive?

Lesson 5.7: America in the 1980s

Political parties became a focus of the American government in the 1980s. The two main political parties were known as **liberals** and **conservatives**. Sometimes these two parties were called "left wing" and "right wing". These are the same as republicans and democrats. Democrats are known as liberal, and republicans are known as conservative.

The basic views of liberals are that the government should provide health insurance for the people, there should be no guns, and there should be welfare (money given to those with low or no income). They also believe that the federal government should govern the people.

The basic views of the conservatives are that the people should provide their own health insurance, the people have a right to have guns, there should be no welfare, and the states should govern the people.

During the 1980s women were used to being in the workforce and for fighting for equal rights. There were protests against the Vietnam War, and women who were liberals felt that women had the right to have an abortion. Conservative women believed the woman's place was in the home taking care of children, the war efforts should be supported, and that abortion was wrong.

Figure 96

Jimmy Carter, a democrat, was elected as President after Richard Nixon resigned. Of course, he inherited all of Nixon's problems such as a troubled economy due to the Vietnam War, and there were some problems with Iran. The liberals who supported him thought that Americans needed to spend more money to get the country out of the economic problems. **OPEC (The Organization of Petroleum Exporting Countries)** embargoed America on oil, which drove the prices way up. This caused many problems including problems with electricity expenses. The economy was in terrible shape.

Ronald Reagan, a conservative, became the next President. He believed that the government should cut the taxes of the rich and that this would help the rich to have more money. They would then create more jobs with their extra money and get more middle and low-income people working. This was called a **trickle-down effect**, and it is known as **Reaganomics.** With the new jobs created, more people would be paying taxes which would fuel the economy. Cutting the taxes of the rich people would encourage them to spend more money. The lower and middle class received some tax cuts, but not as many as the rich. This practice was hotly debated, and it is still debated today as to if it was effective.

Ronald Reagan

Figure 97

Another thing that Ronald Reagan did during his presidency was to deregulate the banks. At this time, the banks could loan money to just about anyone, regardless of credit. He built more nuclear weapons, too. The conservative party helped to bring an end to the Soviet Union and the Berlin wall was torn down.

While the deregulation of the banks helped people to borrow money and spend more, it also meant that the stock market was not being regulated. Some stockbrokers and brokerage firms took advantage of others by saying they were investing their money in retirement funds. Actually, they were pocketing the money for themselves. They were not being regulated, so they were able to do this. Many people became very, very rich in the 80s by doing this, and many people lost their retirement funds as a result.

Even though Reaganomics worked by creating more jobs for the lower and middle class, the jobs did not pay very well. This did not help with spending, because many people in these income classes could not afford to buy much. As a result, the wealth gap between the rich and the poor became bigger and bigger.

Questions:

1.   Why were there problems with the economy when Jimmy Carter took over as President? Explain.

2.   What is another name for the Republican party?

3.   What is another name for the Democratic party?

4.   What were liberal women wanting during the 1980s?

5.   What did conservative women want during the 1980s?

6.   What is OPEC?

7.   Describe Ronald Reagan's idea to generate new jobs for people in the lower and middle class.

8.   What happened when Ronald Reagan deregulated the banking industry in the 80s?

9.   What happened to the Berlin Wall in the 80s?

10.   What did the wealth gap look like at the end of Reagan's presidency?

RESEARCH!

What are some ways that people today are trying to alleviate the problems with OPEC? Create a brief slideshow, poster, or infographic explaining what is happening today and include your opinion on whether or not you think it will work.

Lesson 5.8: Modern Day America

With the fall of the Soviet Union, the Cold War was over. The United States became the lone superpower with China as a close second. The Soviet Union became Russia and a communist country.

Iraq invaded Kuwait in the early 1990s and President **George Bush** started the **Persian-Gulf War** because America depended on Kuwait for oil. Because the entire world relies on **OPEC** (middle eastern countries who export oil) for oil, they sent their militaries to help protect Kuwait from Iraq.

President **Bill Clinton** and his administration saw America continuing to support Israel while working to resolve problems with occupied territories of the Palestinian people. The **PLO**, which is the **Palestinian Liberation Organization** was formed. They gained some power in the 90s and they are still fighting against Israel today. Later in his administration, Bill Clinton was impeached for lying about having sexual relations with an intern named Monica Lewinsky.

In the 2000 Presidential election the Supreme Court had to declare the winner, between **Al Gore** and **George W. Bush**. There was a problem with the voting machines in Florida with little tabs on the paper used for voting. A pin would make little holes to show who someone voted for, but in Florida these holes were hanging pieces of paper. They called these "hanging chads". It took some time, but in the end the Supreme Court had to investigate the hanging chad situation and declare the new President, **George W. Bush.**

Inspecting the hanging chad problem.

Figure 98

174

On September 11, 2001 terrorists from the middle east struck the World Trade Center towers in New York City, and **Osama Bin Laden** was the leader of the terrorist organization responsible for this. **George W. Bush**, president during this time, wanted a war on terror. His administration was responsible for **The Patriot Act**, which said that law enforcement agencies had greater power in gathering information about people. This was supposed to be for monitoring possible terrorists in America, but some thought it was a violation of privacy and went too far. He was also responsible for the **Department of Homeland Security**, which helped to protect America from terrorists.

Figure 99   **The World Trade Center is attacked.**

George W. Bush also told Americans that the leader of Iraq, **Saddam Hussein**, had weapons of mass destruction in Iraq. He called the terrorists *the axis of evil*. America declared war on Iraq to look for these weapons, but they were never found. Hussein was captured and executed.

Barack Obama became the first African American president and his administration was responsible for finding and executing **Osama Bin Laden**, the person responsible for the attacks on the world trade center.

America became a country that talked about peace - world peace. When Ireland and Northern Ireland were fighting, America came in to try to be a peace negotiator. They even got involved in problems that Africa was having. Overall, though, most countries did not want the help of America - they just wanted to be independent.

Questions:

1. What was the Persian-Gulf War about?

2. Why was Bill Clinton impeached?

3. What is a hanging chad, and how did this affect the election between Al Gore and George W. Bush?

4. Who was Osama Bin Laden, and what was he responsible for?

5. What is the Patriot Act?

6. What is the Department of Homeland Security?

7. How did George W. Bush justify the second Persian Gulf War?

8. What is one thing that Barack Obama is known for in his presidency?

9. What has America become known for in modern day history?

10.   Who controls all the oil for the entire world?

WRITE!

In your journal write a list of pros and cons of The Patriot Act. Discuss/debate with a friend or a classmate.

References

Figure 1: Tsiagalakis, George. CC-BY-SA 4. "English: Colonial empires in 1800." Commons.wikimedia.org, 1 November 2014.

Figure 2: Map Thirteen Colonies 1775-fr.svg. "Chart of the Thirteen Colonies of North America before U.S. Independence (around 1775)." Commons.wikimedia.org, 18 October 2012.

Figure 3: The Independent Hall Association in Philadelphia, founded 1942. "Dissent in Massachusetts Bay." www.ushistory.org. Copyright 2008-2021.

Figure 4: Monnpoly, John. Modified by SimonP at en.wikepedia.com. "Depiction of the classical model of the triangular trade." En.wikipedia.org. 21 September 2005. CC BY-SA 30.

Figure 5: Carolinacolony.png. commons.wikimedia.org. 21 June 2013.

Figure 6: Remick, Christian. "The Bloody Massacre". En.wikipedia.org.

Figure 7: Cooper, W.D. "Boston Tea Party in The History of North America." London: E. Newberry, 1789. Engraving. Plate opposite p. 58. Rare Book and Special Collections Edition, Library of Congress. (40).

Figure 8: "Shay's Rebellion". Bettmann Archive/Getty Images. www.thoughtco.com. 2 February, 2022.

Figure 9: "Washington at the Constitutional Convention of 1787, Signing of the U.S. Constitution." www.edsitement.neh.gov Wikimedia Commons. 2 February 2022. **Figure 10:** www.governing.com. Shutterstock. 2 February 2022.

Figure 11: "The Three Branches of Government." www.vannormanlaw.com. 9 January 2016. clients_r3abdv.

Figure 12: "Lame Duck Congress." DonkeyHotey. www.flicker.com/donkey/hotey/8027689882. 26 September, 2012.

Figure 13: "Supreme Court Building." www.aoc.gov. 23 February, 2022.

Figure 14: "The Louisiana Purchase." History.com Editors. www.history.com/topics/westward- expansion/louisiana-purchase 23 February 2022. A&E Television Networks. December 2, 2009.

Figure 15: "1807 Embargo Cartoon". www.commons.wikimedia.org/wiki/File: Ograbme.jpg. 24 February, 2022.

Figure 16: ©Max D. Standley. R. Michelson Galleries. "The Trail of Tears." www.unitedcherokeenation.net/history/the-trail-of -tears. 24 February, 2022.

Figure 17: Gast, John. "American Progress". www.commons.wikimedia.org. 24 February, 2022.

Figure 18: "The Battle of the Alamo." Texas State Archives. www.livescience.com/battle-of- the-alamo. 24 February, 2022.

Figure 19: "Texas State Flag Greetings From the Lone Star State 1940s". www.pinterest.com/pin/74661244477279644. 24 February, 2022.

Figure 20: "Mexican Cession". www.en.wikipedia.org/wiki/Mexican_Cession. 24 February, 2022.

Figure 21: "File: Missouri Compromise Line.svg." www.commons.wikimedia.org/wiki/File: Missouri_Compromise_Line.svg 24 February, 2022.

Figure 22: "Henry Clay". www.nps.gov/people/henry-clay.html. 24 February, 2022. **Figure 23:** "Caning of Charles Sumner." www.en.wikipedia.org/wiki/Caning_of_Charles_Sumner 24 February, 2022

Figure 24: Elliott, J.B. "Scott's Great Snake. Entered according to Act of Congress in the year 1861." www.loc.gov/item/99447020. 24 February, 2022.

Figure 25: Brady, Matthew. "William Tecumseh Sherman". www.en.wikipedia.org/wiki/William_Tecumseh_Sherman. 24 February, 2022.

Figure 26: Klein, Christopher. "10 Things You May Not Know About the Lincoln Assassination." www. History.com/news/10_things_you_may_not_know_about_the_Lincoln_Assassination 24 February, 2022.

Figure 27: Gephardt, Alan. "Murder, Mayhem, Voter Fraud, and Political High Jinks: The U.S. Army's Thankless Task in the South, 1865-77." www.nps.gov. 28 February, 2022.

Figure 28: "Carpetbagger". www.en.wikiepdia.org 28 February, 2022.

Figure 29: "Booker T. Washington". www.en.wikipedia.org. 28 February, 2022.

Figure 30: "W.E.B. DuBois". www.en.wikipedia.org. 28 February, 2022.

Figure 31: "Ida B. Wells Barnett". www.en.wikipedia.org. 28 February, 2022. **Figure 32:** "Marcus Garvey". www.en.wikipedia.org. 28 February, 2022.

Figure 33: "Cultural Impact of Building the Transcontinental Railroad". www.railroad.lindahall.org/essays/cultural-impacts.html 28 February, 2022.

Figure 34: "Sodhouse". www.en.wikipedia.org. 28 February, 2022.

Figure 35: "Building the Transcontinental Railroad". www.pbs.org/wgbh/americanexperience/features/tcrr-gallery/ 28 February, 2022.

Figure 36: Russell, Charles M. "Indians Hunting Buffalo (Wild Men's Meat; Buffalo Hunt)". www.sidrichardsonmuseum.org/where-the-buffalo-roam/ 28 February, 2022.

Figure 37: Vigeant, Fred. "Explore North America's Scenery by Rail." www.witf.org/2021/05/27/explore-north-americas-scenery-by-rail. 28 February, 2022.

Figure 38: "Andrew Carnegie". www.en.wikipedia.org 28 February, 2022.

Figure 39: "John D. Rockefeller". www.en.wikipedia.org. 28 February, 2022.

Figure 40: ©Al Thomas www.parch-mint.com lunarmobiscuit.com/selling-the-first-telephone 1 March, 2022.

Figure 41: "Typewriter". www.sutori.com/en/story/gilded-age-inventions-that-shaped-america. 1 March, 2022.

Figure 42: "Rent strike in Harlem, New York City, September 1919." International Film Service, New York Times photo archive, Public Domain. www.Opendemocracy.net 1 March, 2022. **Figure 43:** Colombo, Matteo. "Little Italy, New York." www.posterlounge.com/p/629005.html 1 March, 2022.

Figure 44: ©Students of History. www.studentsofhistory.com/tenements-urbanization 1 March, 2022.

Figure 45: "Sweatshop". www.en.wikipedia.org/wiki/sweatshop. 1 March, 2022.

Figure 46: "Upton Sinclair". www.en.wikipedia.org/wiki/upton_sinclair. 1 March, 2022.

Figure 47: "World". www.en.wikipedia.org 1 March, 2022.

Figure 48: Public Domain photo. www.militarybyowner.com/hi/joint-base-pearl-harbor-hickam/ 1 March, 2022.

Figure 49: www.flickr.com/photos/timevanson/8754708451. 1 March, 2022.

Figure 50: "karate". www.britannica.com/sports/karate 1 March, 2022.

Figure 51: "Panama Canal". www.en.wikipedia.org 1 March, 2022.

Figure 52: "File: Map Europe Alliances 1914-en.svg". www.commons.wikimedia.org/wiki/File: Map_Europe_alliances_1914-en.svg 1 March, 2022.

Figure 53: "Zimmermann Telegram". www.en.wikipedia.org/wiki/Zimmermann_Telegram 1 March, 2022.

Figure 54: "Food-Guns-Planes-Tanks Quick Buy War Bonds". www.commons.wikimedia.org 1 March, 2022.

Figure 55: "Your Victory Garden". www.commons.wikimedia.org 1 March, 2022.

Figure 56: "Destroy This Mad Brute". www.commons.wikimedia.org 1 March, 2022.

Figure 57: "League of Nations". www.cs.mcgill.ca/~rwest/wikispeedia/wpcs/wp/l/League-of- Nations/htm 1 March, 2022.

Figure 58: "Fascism". www.en.wikipedia.org/wiki/Fascism 1 March, 2022.

Figure 59: "The Ford assembly line in 1913". www.smithsonianmag.com wikimedia commons/public domain. 1 March, 2022.

Figure 60: "The Sacco and Vanzetti Case and its Impact". www.arthurashe.ucla.edu 1 March, 2022.

Figure 61: www.commons.wikimedia.org 8 March 2022.

Figure 62: "King and Carter Jazz Orchestra". www.blackpast.org/african-american- history/harlem-renaissance-american-west. 8 March, 2022.

Figure 63: "18 Details in the Daily Life of a Bootlegger During Prohibition." www.historycollection.com Library of Congress. 8 March, 2022.

Figure 64: www.commons.wikimedia.org 8 March, 2022.

Figure 65: "Tracing poignant, heroic last days of FDR." www.bostonglobe.com FDR Library. 8 March, 2022.

Figure 66: "When Stalin Invited Bhagat Singh to Soviet Union." www.newsclick.in 8 March, 2022.

Figure 67: "Death of the Duce, Benito Mussolini." www.nationalww2museum.org 8 March, 2022.

Figure 68: "Politician Named after Adolph Hitler Wins Election In Namibia." www.africanews.com 8 March, 2022.

Figure 69: "Hideki Tojo." www.enwikipedia.org 8 March, 2022.

Figure 70: "First Peacetime Draft Enacted Just Before World War II." www.defense.gov 8 March, 2022.

Figure 71: "Attack on Pearl Harbor." www.en.wikipedia.org 8 March, 2022.

Figure 72: "Keep Talking I'm All Ears" NARA-514812.jpg www.wikimedia.org 8 March, 2022. **Figure 73:** "Together we can do it." Public Domain. www.allaboutlean.com 8 March, 2022. **Figure 74:** "Rosie the Riveter." National Archives/Getty Images. www.history.com 8 March, 2022.

Figure 75: "File: Sample UK Child's Ration Book WW2.jpg." www.en.wikipedia.org 8 March, 2022.

Figure 76: "File: Keep this Horror From Your Home. Invest 10 Percent in War Bonds Back Up our Battleskies" – NARA-534105.jpg www.commons.wikimedia.org 8 March, 2022.

Figure 77: "Family Separation Is Being Compared to Japanese Internment. It Took Decades for the U.S. to Admit That Policy Was Wrong." www.time.com 8 March, 2022.

Figure 78: "Yalta Conference." www.en.wikipedia.org 8 March, 2022.

Figure 79: "George Patton." www.en.wikepedia.org 14 March, 2022.

Figure 80: "D-Day." www.en.wikipedia.org. 14 March, 2022.

Figure 81: Britannica, The Editors of Encyclopedia. "Tuskegee Airmen." Encyclopedia Britannica, 24 Jan. 2020, https://www.britannica.com/topic/Tuskegee-Airmen.

Figure 82: "Geography of Japan." www.en.wikipedia.org 14 March, 2022.

Figure 83: www.thehawkeye.com/story/news/history/2020/08/06/hiroshima-75th-anniversary-iowa-pilot-paul-tibets-flew-enola-gay-that-dropped-bomb/1128985 14 March, 2022.

Figure 84: "microwave oven invention". www.en.wikipedia.org 14 March, 2022.

Figure 85: www.dallasnews.com/arts-entertainment/books/2018/06/20/concentration-camps-didn-t-start-or-end-with-nazi-germany-one-long-night-is-their-history 14 March, 2022.

Figure 86: "Israeli-occupied territories." www.en.wikepedia.org 15 March, 2022.

Figure 87: Fischer, Gregor/dpa via Getty Images. www.news.artnet.com/art-world/berlin-wall- destroyed-pankow-1822947 15 March, 2022

Figure 88: www.commons.wikimedia.org/wiki-FileArchibald-Neil-Sinclair-house-bomb-shelter.JPG 15 March, 2022

Figure 89: "MacDill Air Force Base Commentaries." www.macdill.af.mil/News/Commentaries/Article/17344641/continuing-the-dream-of-dr- martin-luther-king-jr/ 15 March, 2022

Figure 90: "Washington Area Spark". www.flickr.com/photos/washington_area_spark/50112735118 15 March, 2022

Figure 91: "Johnson Takes Oath of Office Aboard Air Force One." www.history.com/topics/us- presidents-johnson-takes-oath-of-office-aboard-air-force-one-video 15 March, 2022.

Figure 92: "Ho Chi Minh in Newhaven: From Pastry Chef in East Sussex to Patriotic Leader of Vietnam." www.independent.co.uk/news/uk/home-news/ho-chi-minh-in-newhaven-from- pastry-chef-in-East-Sussex-to-Patriotic-Leader-of-Vietnam-10157622. 15 March, 2022.

Figure 93: "Map of the Ho Chi Minh Trail." www.photos.com/featured/map-of-the-ho-chi- minh-trail-bettmann.html 16 March, 2022.

Figure 94: "USA/Vietnam: 'Get The Hell Out of Vietnam'. Anti Vietnam War Protest, Washington, DC, 21 October 1967. www.bridgemanimages.com image number PFH3277836 15 March, 2022.

Figure 95: www.history.com/this-day-in-history/nixon-resigns 16 March, 2022.

Figure 96: "Abortion Stays in the Spotlight in Courts, State Legislatures." www.medpagetoday.com/obgyn/pregnancy/94192 16 March, 2022.

Figure 97: "Ronald Reagan." www.en.wikipedia.org 16 March, 2022.

Figure 98: "Hanging Chads, lawsuits and the Supreme Court: NBC podcast looks at 2000 election." www.tallhassee.com/story/news/2020/10/B 16 March, 2022.

Figure 99: Platt, Spencer "Why an attack like 0/11 is much less likely today than it was in 2001". www.vox.com/2016/9/9/128398241 16 March, 2022.

Meet my teaching partner, Richard Bonneville

Richard Bonneville is a graduate of The Citadel (The Military College of South Carolina) with a B.S. in Education and a concentration in Social Studies. He also holds a master's degree in Leadership and Administration and is a National Board-Certified teacher with over 24 years of experience at the secondary level. With his experience teaching struggling learners, he has learned what it takes to meet the unique challenges that his students face and has developed highly effective teaching strategies that he is known and much loved for. Together with his teaching partner, Julie Collins, they have developed a powerful U.S. History curriculum that is both meaningful and fun for exceptional students. Mr. Bonneville has a passion for teaching History, and he loves high school sports. He is happily married to the beautiful Leah Caldwell Bonneville from Columbia, South Carolina. Together they have two wonderful sons and two dogs named Sampson and Penny Lane.

Meet the Graphic Designer, Courtney Steele Welcome

Courtney (Steele) Welcome was born in Germany and called many places home before realizing Savannah, Georgia was the one place that was truly home. She always knew she had a passion for creative outlets, but it wasn't until joining her high school newspaper and literary magazine that she found her true passion: digital art.

Courtney went on to attend High Tech North in Cape Coral, Florida where she earned a certificate in Digital Design. She loves challenging herself with custom logo designs and branding as well as acrylic paintings, murals, and tattoo designs. In her free time Courtney enjoys spending time with her family, friends, and 3 pets: Cooper, Lady, and Freyja. Connect with Courtney on social media to view more of her work @courtney.steele.art

Author Notes

Several years ago, Julie Collins, (ESOL teacher) was approached by her school administrators to consider a co-teaching assignment with Richard Bonneville, (U.S. History teacher). The idea was for them to collaborate in a shared classroom to design a way to make the U.S. History curriculum accessible to ESOL students taking the course. The experience proved to be the most challenging and rewarding work of their careers and resulted in the creation of this workbook. Over the years they improved their instruction and created materials as they developed a brand-new curriculum that not only enabled ESOL students to soar, but also helped so many other students. It was a great deal of work, fun, and frustration, but ultimately resulted in a deep friendship and a lot of joy. They are excited to be able to share this with you!

Julie met Courtney on Wilmington Island near her home in Savannah, Georgia and began to collaborate ideas for the book cover design. Many, many meetings took place as the two made decisions for the cover. Ultimately, the result is a map that represents some of the important people and events in United States History. Courtney was able to design a cover that is a visual lesson in U.S. History! Can you name all the important icons on the cover? Can you give even more information than names about each icon on the cover? See how many you can guess and check your answers below!

KEY: (top right, clockwise) twin towers, Mayflower, The U.S. Constitution, Dr. Martin Luther King, Jr., The Citadel, plantation, The U.S.S. Maine, Theodore Roosevelt, Zimmerman Note, World War II Japanese planes, The Mexican War or Mexican-American War, The Alamo, Bison/Buffalo and Native Americans or Indian Wars, tee-pees, gold/iron/coal mining in California, bison/buffalo, Prohibition era, factories (middle of map, down) transcontinental railroad, Manifest Destiny angel, scalawag, carpetbagger

Made in the USA
Coppell, TX
15 August 2023

20384032R00109